ENGLISH in Common

Workbook

Antonia Clare and JJ Wilson

Series Consultants
María Victoria Saumell and Sarah Louisa Birchley

PEARSON

English in Common 6
Workbook

Pearson Education, 10 Bank Street, White Plains, NY 10606

Staff credits: The editorial, design, production, and
manufacturing people who make up the *English in Common 6*
team are Margaret Antonini, Allen Ascher, Rhea Banker, Eleanor
Kirby Barnes, Peter Benson, Tracey Cataldo, Aerin Csigay, Mindy
DePalma, Dave Dickey, Chris Edmonds, Mike Kemper, Jessica
Miller-Smith, Laurie Neaman, Daria Ruzicka, Loretta Steeves, Jeff
Zeter, and Charlie Green.

This series is dedicated to Charlie Green. Without Charlie's
knowledge of pedagogy, strong work ethic, sense of humor,
patience, perseverance, and creativity, *English in Common* would
never have existed.

Cover design: Tracey Cataldo
Cover photo: © qushe/shutterstock.com
Text design: Tracey Cataldo
Text composition: TSI Graphics
Text font: MetaPlus

ISBN 13: 978-0-13-267896-4
ISBN 10: 0-13-267896-9

Library of Congress Cataloging-in-Publication Data
Bygrave, Jonathan
    English in common. Book 1 / Jonathan Bygrave.
        p. cm.
ISBN 0-13-247003-9—ISBN 0-13-262725-6—
ISBN 0-13-262727-2—ISBN 0-13-262728-0—
ISBN 0-13-262729-9—ISBN 0-13-262731-0
1. English language—Textbooks for foreign speakers.
2. English language—Grammar.
3. English language—Spoken English.
    PE1128.B865 2011
    428.24—dc23

2011024736

Printed in the United States of America
1 2 3 4 5 6 7 8 9 10—V001—16 15 14 13 12

Text Credits: Excerpt from "Mine" on page 80 reprinted with
permission of Allen Ascher.

Photo Credits: All photos are ©Pearson Education except for
the following. Page 4 Simon Fergusson/Getty Images;
p. 6 Shutterstock.com; p. 7 Shutterstock.com; p. 9
Shutterstock.com; p. 12 (all) Shutterstock.com; p. 16 (left)
Peter Horree/Alamy, (top right) Sami Sarkis Travel/Alamy,
(bottom right) Shutterstock.com; p. 17 Shutterstock.com;
p. 19 Shutterstock.com; p. 20 Shutterstock.com; p. 22
Shutterstock.com; p. 27 Shutterstock.com; p. 28 (left)
AF archive/Alamy, (right) Photos 12/Alamy, (bottom)
AF archive/Alamy; p. 30 Shutterstock.com; p. 32 Ami Vitale/
Getty Images; p. 36 Shutterstock.com; p. 37 Shutterstock.com;
p. 43 Shutterstock.com; p. 44 Shutterstock.com; p. 46
Shutterstock.com; p. 52 PA Photos/Landov; p. 54 (all)
Shutterstock.com; p. 55 Shutterstock.com; p. 56
Shutterstock.com; p. 58 Shutterstock.com; p. 61
Shutterstock.com; p. 62 Shutterstock.com; p. 66
Shutterstock.com; p. 71 Time & Life Pictures/Getty Images;
p. 73 Creatas/Punchstock; p. 74 Joe Raedle/Getty Images;
p. 80 Shutterstock.com; p. 83 Shutterstock.com.

Illustration Credits: Roger Penwill, Brian Lee and Lucy Truman
(New Division)

Contents

A **Workbook Answer Key** is provided on *ActiveTeach* at the back of the Teacher's Resource Book. Click on the Printable Resources tab at the bottom of the screen.

Achieving goals

Reading

1a Read the article. What makes Mark Inglis unusual?

_____

_____

Testing the Limits

On May 15, 2006, a boyhood dream came true for Mark Inglis, a mountain climber from New Zealand. He had always wanted to stand on the roof of the world. At the age of 47, he became the first man with two artificial legs to reach the summit of Mount Everest, the highest mountain in the world at 29,092 feet (8,848 meters).

In 1982, as a search and rescue mountain guide, Mark was trapped in a blizzard for two weeks on Mount Cook, the highest mountain in New Zealand. Both legs were amputated due to frostbite. After recovering, Mark went on to become a medical scientist in leukemia research, a winemaker, and an inspiring motivational speaker.

Being a double amputee has never slowed him down. He has been able to ski and has always loved cycling. He won a silver medal in cycling in the 2000 Sydney Paralympic games. He then returned to that same mountain where he lost his legs to finish the climb he started twenty years ago.

After conquering Mount Cook, he went on to climb Mount Cho Oyu in Tibet, the world's sixth highest peak at 26,901 feet (8,201 meters). From the summit of Cho Oyu, he looked out at Everest and decided that would be his next challenge. He was able to make the climb on two carbon-fiber artificial legs, designed especially for climbing. One of his artificial limbs snapped on the way up the mountain, but he was able to repair it quickly with the tools and the spare leg parts he had brought with him.

Though his voice was shaky and it was difficult to speak on the top of Mount Everest, he was able to call his wife Anne and share his great news. She said, "He's dreamed of this all his life . . . "

Helen Clark, the New Zealand Prime Minister, also an amateur climber, officially congratulated Mark for his great accomplishment. She said that he had sent a message to other people with disabilities "that your ambitions should never be limited."

Because of the Everest climb he was able to raise tens of thousands of dollars for the Cambodia Trust, an organization that helps amputees. Recently he created a new charity called Limbs4All, which is working to help 400 million disabled people in the world.

b Mark the sentences true (*T*) or false (*F*).

____ 1. Mark Inglis had both legs amputated due to frostbite in 1982.

____ 2. He never found the courage to return to climb the mountain where he lost his legs.

____ 3. On reaching the top of Everest, Mark was completely unable to speak.

____ 4. The Prime Minister of New Zealand congratulated Mark on his achievement.

____ 5. Mark broke one of his artificial legs while climbing down the mountain.

____ 6. Mark successfully climbed Mount Cook and Mount Cho Oyu before attempting Mount Everest.

____ 7. Before his legs were amputated Mark had also won a silver medal for cycling.

2a Complete the questions with words from the box.

make	set	ambition	rising
without	face	attitude	

1. What achievable goals did Mark _____?

2. What challenges did he _____?

3. Did Mark succeed in _____ to the challenge?

4. How did he _____ his dream come true?

5. What couldn't Mark have done it _____?

6. What advice did the Prime Minister give to people with an ultimate _____?

7. Do you think Mark had the right _____?

b Answer the questions in Exercise 2a on a separate sheet of paper.

Grammar

3 Circle the correct choice.

1. We finally opted *to/for/on* the silver color.
2. It is a method of distinguishing cancer cells *from/between/of* normal tissue.
3. Very few people succeed *on losing/to lose/in losing* weight and keeping it off.
4. His headaches stemmed *from/with/to* vision problems.
5. It is most likely to appeal *at/to/with* the younger generation.
6. We all came to rely *on/in/with* her judgment.
7. We want him to get the maximum benefit *of/from/with* the class.
8. The wall of the prison was riddled *of/in/with* bullet holes.
9. She seems to be lacking *with/on/in* confidence.

Vocabulary

4 Complete the conversations with words from the box.

> delight   cram   master
> picked   linguistic ability

1. **A:** I didn't know you could speak Thai!
   B: I can't really. I just _____ up a few words while I was there on vacation.
2. **A:** How long did it take you to _____ the grammar?
   B: Years! I had to _____ a lot of information into my brain.
3. **A:** What do you enjoy most about being able to speak Russian?
   B: The sheer _____ of being able to talk to people I meet there.
4. **A:** I can't believe how quickly she's learned the language.
   B: Yes, she has an amazing _____ .

Reading

5 Read the article. Then answer the questions on a separate sheet of paper.

Languages and the brain

Research has shown that people with a gift for languages could actually have different types of brains from other people.

In a recent trial involving native French speakers, people were asked to distinguish between two similar sounds from different languages. The first was the /d/ sound found in French. The second was a /d/ found in Hindi, which is pronounced in a different way. Researchers tested the speed at which participants could process the information about the different sounds. People who were successful in this task were asked to listen to other similar sounds.

Some of the fastest learners were able to tell the sounds apart within a few minutes, while the slowest learners were only able to make random guesses after 20 minutes of training.

Dr. Narly Golestani, from the University College London's Institute of Cognitive Neuroscience, said the brain's white matter was involved in the efficient processing of sound information. Its fibers are involved in connecting brain regions together. Fast language learners had a greater volume of white matter, and that may mean they have more, or perhaps thicker, fibers.

"We are starting to understand that brain shape and structure can be informative about people's abilities—why people are good at some things and not others is evident from these scans," she said.

"This latest research could be used in other ways," Dr. Golestani said. "We can start to make predictions regarding whether people will be good at something or not based on their brain structure or even to diagnose clinical problems."

1. What do scientists hope to achieve through the new research?
2. What did people have to distinguish between during the trial?
3. How did the researchers decide who was a "good" language learner?
4. What is the function of fibers in the brain's white matter?
5. What can you tell from the brain scans?

Vocabulary

1 Match the beginning of the sentence with its end.

____ 1. We had to learn poems by	a. head, I'd say there were about 50.
____ 2. I grew up here. I know it like the back	b. of my hand.
____ 3. I know next to	c. David Marshall?
____ 4. Just off the top of my	d. heart when I was in school.
____ 5. I'm pretty	e. what time the show starts?
____ 6. Have you ever heard of	f. sure he'll say yes.
____ 7. Lee knew the game	g. nothing about antiques.
____ 8. Do you know offhand	h. inside out.

Grammar

2 Read the article. Underline examples of passives and other verbs used for distancing.

Notable lasts

1. Lillian Asplund, who died at age 99, was the last American survivor of the Titanic, and the only living person with any memory of the events of April 15, 1912. She was five years old when the ship went down in the freezing waters of the north Atlantic, taking with it her father and three of her brothers. As she was pulled to safety in a lifeboat, she saw them peering at her over the ship's railing. The image is said to have haunted her for the rest of her life, and despite the world's ongoing fascination with the Titanic, it seems she rarely spoke of the tragedy.

2. Martha is thought to have been the last surviving passenger pigeon. Passenger pigeons were probably once the most common bird in the world. It is estimated that there were as many as five billion passenger pigeons in the United States. They lived in enormous flocks, sometimes up to a mile wide and 300 miles long, taking several days to pass and probably containing two billion birds. They were hunted to extinction by humans. Martha, the last of her species, died in the Cincinnati Zoo in 1914. She was then frozen in a block of ice and her body was sent to The Smithsonian Institution, where she can still be seen.

3. Ishi was the name given to the last member of the Yahi tribe of California, and means "man" in the Yahi language. Ishi is believed to be the last Native American in Northern California to have lived the bulk of his life completely outside the European American culture. He was thought to have left his homeland in the foothills near Lassen Peak, California, and was found when he emerged from the wild on August 29, 1911. His real name was never known, because in his society it was taboo to say one's own name. Since he was the last member of his tribe, his real name died with him.

3 Complete the paragraphs using passives and the verbs in parentheses. Add extra words if necessary.

It _____ (1. say) that Thomas Edison, the famous inventor, believed that taking off one's clothing caused insomnia. It _____ (2. seem) that he often slept in his clothes on newspapers beneath the stairs in his laboratory.

Alexander Graham Bell, inventor of the telephone, _____ (3. claim) to have first answered the device by saying "hoy, hoy" instead of "hello"!

Charles Goodyear, who _____ (4. say) to have been instrumental in establishing the rubber industry in the US, _____ (5. think) to have carried out his first experiments in jail.

Leonardo da Vinci _____ (6. think) to have designed a military tank in the fifteenth century. Remarkably, he _____ (7. believe) to have also worked on designs for hot-air balloons and deep-sea diving suits.

Joseph Merlin, a Belgian musician, invented roller skates in 1760. He _____ (8. appear) to have first demonstrated them at a ball by skating across the room playing a violin.

Reading

4a Read the news clippings. Circle the key words.

For the second year in a row, the city of Luanda, Angola, has beaten Tokyo for the title of "world's most expensive city." The city is pricey because there is little competition and few items are produced locally. Interestingly, although Luanda is very expensive, over half of the Angolan population lives in poverty.

Crime in many US cities, including Washington D.C., has decreased in recent years. Local authorities credit better policing and technology for the drop. Thanks to mobile technology, law enforcement can receive up-to-date reports on criminal activity and emergencies in their patrol areas. In D.C., this has resulted in the lowest crime rates in forty years.

Tourism officials are reminding visitors to China to be vigilant and to keep an eye on their surroundings and belongings. This warning comes after video surveillance caught several Chinese pickpockets stealing wallets and cell phones using chopsticks. These bold thieves target inattentive passersby and dip into their pockets with the wooden utensils.

Teens in some parts of Philadelphia are now subject to a 9:00 P.M. curfew. The curfew was established because groups of teens have been harassing other citizens and disturbing local businesses. These groups have been organizing their criminal acts using text messaging and social media websites like Twitter and Facebook.

b Answer the questions on a separate sheet of paper.
1. How can the lack of locally-made products drive up prices in a city?
2. How do you think police can use technology to prevent crime?
3. What are some ways to keep your belongings safe from pickpockets?
4. What are some good and bad uses for social media?

Reading

1a Read the interview on the right. Then answer the questions.

1. What kinds of races does Annie compete in?
2. What is her ambition?
3. How did her parents influence her?
4. What injuries has she suffered?
5. How does she cope when she is hurt?

b Find words or expressions in the reading that mean:

1. only just (paragraph 1) _____
2. something she really wants to achieve (paragraph 2) _____
3. be an equally strong competitor (paragraph 2) _____
4. be very eager to do something (paragraph 4) _____
5. be able to do (paragraph 5) _____
6. give up (paragraph 6) _____

c Complete the sentences. Use the correct form of the words and phrases from Exercise 1b.

1. He is extremely ambitious. His _____ is to take over the whole company.
2. My job is getting so stressful, I'm thinking about _____ .
3. They had _____ exited the office when the police arrived.
4. The Mexican team is very talented and will prove to be a _____ for the Canadians.
5. I was _____ for an adventure, so I signed up for a trip across Africa.
6. I'm not sure that they're entirely _____ finishing the job.

Nerves of steel

(1) She's blond, charming, enthusiastic, and above all, extremely determined. If you judge Annie Seel only by her looks, you're in for the greatest of surprises. There are other women motorcyclists for sure, but how many crave extreme adventure in such a way, and how many single-handedly take on all the toughest rallies the world has to offer? Addicted early on to speed and adrenaline, the desert princess switched from horses to motorcycle races when she was barely 16.

(2) After 20 years and 17 broken bones, she continues to try to quench her thirst for success and for new records to break, as much at home up Mount Everest as on African rallies, on tarmac races as on Mexican bajas. Can you guess the ultimate quest for this woman? To be a true match for her male counterparts in the greatest races, starting with a race called the Rallye du Maroc, in which she's riding in the marathon class.

(3) **Annie, what gave you this taste for extreme adventure?**

"I grew up next to a racecourse. I quickly got addicted to speed, and then at 16, I saw some motorcycle stuntmen at a show. I was awed. I bought myself a motorcycle, but none of my friends liked speed as much as I did. Then, when I was 18, I started to do road racing and finished eighth in the Swedish Championships . . ."

(4) **And in 2000 you tried a rally in Dubai . . .**

"I went to Morocco and fell in love with the desert. I was desperate to do a race. I ordered a DIY Husaberg 600 and assembled it barely ten days before the start.

(5) I rode on my own and made straight for the sand dunes. On the last day, I got a fractured foot but I still got to the finish in 49th place. Since then, I've been to Tunisia and Argentina. This Moroccan race is my sixth one in the World Championships. I'm trying to show what I'm capable of doing with the hope of finding some money for the Dakar race. To tell you the truth, it's fairly hard to find any money in Sweden for these kinds of races . . ."

(6) **What's most impressive about you is your determination. You've broken your bones 17 times, yet you've never given up.**

"No, I never quit. My father, who died when I was 16, gave me a taste for mechanical things, and my mother gave me exceptionally strong will power. When I broke my hand on the fourth stage of the Dakar in 2002, I held on until the end. My left leg had gone blue all over. I'll admit, though, that I've always been lucky enough to have injuries that didn't prevent me from finishing the race. When I run into a problem, I scream a little and then I go on."

Vocabulary

2 Complete the sentences with words from the box.

> pushing   faces   pursue   heading   deal

1. You need to keep your priorities straight if you want to _____ your dream.
2. The president _____ the difficult task of putting the economy back on its feet.
3. My tutor was always _____ me to do better.
4. We have had to _____ with a lot of unnecessary criticism.
5. I'm worried they may be _____ for trouble.

Grammar

3 Complete the article using the correct form of the verbs in parentheses.

Dutch motorcycle rider Martin Jansen is a very calm and patient man. By the end of this year he _____ (**1.** be) on the road for over 30 years. This hardworking and determined biker, who _____ (**2.** travel) a quarter of a million miles, through 100 different countries, arrived in Vancouver last week. Shortly after arriving on the ferry from the Granville Islands, the motorcycle that _____ (**3.** be) his constant companion for 30 years was stolen. However, Martin took it in stride. After all, he couldn't _____ (**4.** spend) all those years riding around the world without learning a little patience.

Actually, his motorcycle _____ (**5.** be returned) to him just 24 hours after its theft. Jansen somehow knew he would get it back. Before this, the bike _____ already _____ (**6.** be stolen) on three previous occasions. The last time _____ (**7.** be) in 2000. He thinks that having your motorcycle stolen almost every ten years is not too bad, considering how long he _____ (**8.** be) traveling.

This is not the only problem Jansen _____ (**9.** have) to deal with. Since he _____ (**10.** give up) his job as an auto mechanic in Pennsylvania and set off on his journey, Jansen _____ (**11.** be hit) three times by cars, and _____ even _____ (**12.** break) both legs. He earns money by writing and selling books about his travels. But he _____ often _____ (**13.** be) hungry. His life has been an incredible experience, and he is looking forward to many more adventures.

Writing

4 Write a paragraph about a personal achievement or about another person's achievement that you particularly admire. Use a separate sheet of paper.

> **Ideas:**
> career   health
> family   travel
> sports   school
> fulfilling a dream

1 Circle the correct word or phrase to complete each sentence.

1. It is widely ____ eating too many fatty foods causes heart disease.
   - a. believing
   - b. to be believed of
   - c. believed that
   - d. believed to be

2. The notes from last month's meeting ____ lost.
   - a. are appeared
   - b. seem to have be
   - c. appear that they are
   - d. seem to have been

3. It seems ____ Mr. Klein was wrong about the figures.
   - a. that
   - b. if
   - c. as to
   - d. as

4. Is the shipment ____ this afternoon?
   - a. be delivered
   - b. being delivered
   - c. deliver
   - d. to deliver

5. Smoking ____ allowed on planes for years.
   - a. isn't being
   - b. isn't
   - c. hasn't been
   - d. doesn't

6. ____ in the past that the world was flat?
   - a. Was there assumed
   - b. Did it assume
   - c. Was assumed
   - d. Was it assumed

7. Carlos ____ the most handsome man in Buenos Aires society.
   - a. has said to be
   - b. was said to be
   - c. was to be
   - d. was said

8. The company ____ gone bankrupt because of increased competition.
   - a. is thought
   - b. is said to be
   - c. said to have
   - d. is thought to have

2 Match the beginning of the sentence with its end.

____ 1. She is said to
____ 2. It was widely
____ 3. The robbers were thought
____ 4. Judging by this map, we appear to have
____ 5. It seems as though
____ 6. You look as
____ 7. The competition entry must
____ 8. The wedding cake will have been

- a. made by now.
- b. if you've just seen a ghost.
- c. to have escaped.
- d. be a genius.
- e. be submitted by tomorrow.
- f. the weather will get better.
- g. become completely lost.
- h. assumed that Minsoo would inherit his father's money.

3 Complete each sentence using the correct perfect form of the verb in parentheses.

1. By this time next week we _____ school, and I'll be on vacation! (finish)

2. It was only when Mariana told me her name that I realized we _____ before. (meet)

3. The children were all sunburned. They _____ football in the sun all day. (play)

4. She looks exhausted because she _____ well recently. (not sleep)

5. By next July, Kazunari probably _____ his thesis. (write)

6. Yesterday, Mr. Jones finally received his visa. He _____ to get one for years. (try)

7. Wow! Fantastic news! I _____ a scholarship to the university. (win)

8. We went to a Mowgli concert. I _____ of them before, but they were very good. (not hear)

9. By tomorrow, Don _____ here for over fifty years! He started as an assistant. (be)

4 Is the sentence in *italics* replying to statement **a** or **b**?

1. a. We haven't been feeding the cat enough food.
   b. We haven't fed the cat enough food.
   ____ *I know. He's started catching mice again recently.*

2. a. How many countries will you have visited after this trip?
   b. How many countries will you visit on this trip?
   ____ *If you include the one where I was born, then 18!*

3. a. We haven't been told the schedule.
   b. We hadn't been told the schedule.
   ____ *Well, I think the conference starts at 9:00, and you're speaking at 11:00.*

4. a. I've been sitting quietly, minding my own business.
   b. I'd been sitting quietly, minding my own business.
   ____ *And then what happened?*

5. a. Where have you put the money?
   b. Where will you have put the money?
   ____ *I put it where you told me to.*

5 Complete the article with the correct form of words from the box plus a preposition.

opt	appeal	succeed	benefit
rely	bother	nervous	
short	subject	reminiscent	

Vacation challenge

Vacation Challenge is guaranteed to _____ (1.) your adventurous spirit. We provide a choice of parachute jumps, hang gliding, rock climbing and kayaking. You can _____ (2.) two sports plus luxury accommodations and food for just $300 a week! Or, if you're _____ (3.) cash, you can choose the economy camping option for $175.

What if you are _____ (4.) trying a new sport? Don't worry. You can _____ (5.) us to provide the best training available to ensure that you're safe. And we won't _____ you _____ (6.) any 5:00 A.M. mornings or boot camp horrors! Read what our customers have said about us.

"I really _____ (7.) my two weeks with Vacation Challenge. It was an amazing experience!" (*Cal Jones, New York*)

"It was _____ (8.) my childhood: running around, learning new stuff, without a care in the world. The best vacation I've ever had." (*Young-Chul, Korea*)

"Don't _____ (9.) checking the competitors. Vacation Challenge is the one." (*Sanath Kuppara, Sri Lanka*)

"I _____ (10.) living my dreams! Thank you, Vacation Challenge." (*Macarena Duval, Chile*)

6 Add or cross out one word to complete each sentence.

1. Paulo Freire? Who's he? I've never heard him.
2. The Whorf-Sapir hypothesis? I know it like in the back of my hand.
3. Wendy's phone number? I don't know it by offhand.
4. Shakespeare's love poems? We spent years learning them by the heart.
5. Rules in the driving manual? Ask Susie—she's a driving instructor. She knows it inside.
6. International banking? I know next nothing about it.

7 Number the lines 1–11 to put them in the correct order.

_1_ Climber Rheinhold Messner always knew that he had the

____ challenge. Most doctors and scientists suggested that this was not an achievable

____ come true with a successful three-day ascent.

____ all expectations. After a few months' preparation, Messner pursued his dream

____ something truly amazing in the mountains. However, in 1980, he exceeded

____ of risk about climbing Everest, but Messner's attempt to take

____ of being the first man to ascend Everest without oxygen supplies. There is always an element

____ potential to accomplish

____ on the world's highest mountain without

____ goal. Against all expectations, on August 20, he made his dream

____ oxygen was a real

UNIT 2
Places and communities

LESSON 1

Communication

1a Read about three students' embarrassing moments abroad. Complete the chart.

	Speaker 1	Speaker 2	Speaker 3
1. Nationality of speaker			
2. Country where embarrassing moment happened			
3. Main problem			
4. Speaker's final thoughts about the situation			

Embarrassing moments

Speaker 1

After a long journey from Vancouver, I was really happy to have arrived at my host family's house in Colombia. They were extremely friendly, even though I spoke only a little Spanish, and they plied me with lemonade and made me feel comfortable. After a while, the mother asked me, "Estas casado"? I thought she was asking me if I was tired, so I said: "Si, un poco," which means "yes, a little." Suddenly everyone laughed. Later I found out that "casado" means married, and "cansado" means tired. So she'd asked me if I was married and I'd said: "Oh, a little"! That was just the first of many linguistic blunders I made! Actually, looking back, I wish I'd learned more of the language before moving there, but I did pick it up pretty quickly.

Speaker 2

I'm from Argentina, but I've lived in the US for ten years. When I first got a car, I needed to buy gas, so I drove to a gas station and sat there waiting to be served. And I sat there, and I sat there, and no one came. Eventually, a little perplexed, I went into the store and asked for a full tank of gas. The girl took my money, and I went back to the car and waited again. Still, no one came.

So I thought maybe someone had done it for me while I was in the store. So I drove off. But then I looked at the gas gauge and the tank was completely empty. I drove back to the gas station and suddenly I realized I had to fill the car myself. I've never done this before, because in Argentina the people who work at the gas station do it for you. I felt a little bit stupid, as you can imagine.

Speaker 3

This was before I could speak English well. I was flying back to Italy, and I was at JFK Airport. For some reason, I didn't have my glasses. I'm very short sighted so I couldn't see the information on the screen. So I asked someone official-looking, "Which gate for Milan?" and he said: "It's too early. There's no gate." I got confused because I thought that "early" meant "late," so I began to panic, thinking I'd missed my flight. So I asked someone else, and again: "You're too early. No gate assigned. You'll have to wait." And I was tearing my hair out and wondering why these Americans were so calm when I'd just missed my flight. Eventually, a nice American man explained, very pleasantly, that the gate number would appear very soon and that I hadn't missed my flight. He was probably thinking: "Dumb tourist." So the moral of the story is: learn the basics. And don't lose your glasses!

b Find words or phrases in the reading that mean:

1. give someone large amounts of food or drink (Speaker 1) _____
2. careless mistakes (Speaker 1) _____
3. confused by something (Speaker 2) _____
4. formal word for *given*, for example, a task or a seat (Speaker 3) _____
5. idiom for going crazy or getting angry (Speaker 3) _____

Grammar

2 Circle the correct choice.

1. The travel agency recommends _to take/ taking/take_ traveler's checks rather than cash.

2. We look forward to _meet/meeting/have met_ you in June.

3. My parents always encouraged me _that write/ writing/to write_ down my thoughts.

4. After graduating, Melissa thought _of travel/ of traveling/to travel_ for a year, but decided against it.

5. Mark recommended _ride/her to ride/riding_ a bicycle as a good way to get in shape.

6. They couldn't afford _to waste/that they waste/wasting_ time on trivial matters.

7. I would urge _to reconsider/you to reconsider/ you reconsider_ the offer before it's too late.

8. We've avoided _to do/that we do/doing_ anything too dangerous so far.

9. I object _I have to/to having to/I have to_ pay for my own travel to these conferences.

10. Chiara persuaded _us that we go/us go/us to go_ on a boat trip with her.

3 Match the beginning of the sentence with its end.

____ 1. The Taj Mahal really is a must-

____ 2. Disney World is a superb value

____ 3. The hotel is nice, but it's

____ 4. Everyone says the museum is amazing, but in my view it's not

____ 5. If I were you, I'd

____ 6. You should try

____ 7. Make sure

____ 8. Watch out

a. for mosquitoes, and take your malaria pills.

b. backpacking because it's cheap.

c. see because it's so beautiful.

d. all it's cracked up to be.

e. go in April, when it isn't too hot.

f. a little overpriced.

g. you go to Macchu Pichu.

h. for the money.

4 Complete the article using the correct form of verbs from the box. Add extra words where necessary.

try	hear	make	object	find out
live	think	advise	afford	change

Culture shock

Those people thinking _____ (**1.**) abroad will face a number of challenges, including communication difficulties and settling in to a new community. But perhaps the biggest challenge is culture shock. You may find yourself _____ (**2.**) to everything about the host culture: the way the people drive, wait in line, greet you, their habits, and attitudes toward everything around you, such as litter and personal space. This is common. People cannot avoid _____ (**3.**) that their own culture does things "the right way." Everything else is therefore wrong. We urge you _____ (**4.**) your mindset. There are no cultural rights or wrongs, only differences. What's more, if you're committed to staying in a foreign country for more than a few days, you can't _____ (**5.**) be critical of everything around you. It'll make your life miserable.

The greatest divider of nations is ignorance, and so the first solution is knowledge. We recommend _____ (**6.**) as much as you can about the host culture before you arrive—its customs, people, priorities, and manners. When you've done your homework, if you really can't imagine _____ (**7.**) a new life there, go somewhere else.

We also encourage you _____ (**8.**) to see that diversity is interesting. No one would really want to live in a world in which every culture was the same, so we _____ (**9.**) you to observe and enjoy the differences. Eventually you will come to accept them.

We look forward _____ (**10.**) from you about your experiences.

5 Make the sentences more polite using the words in parentheses.

1. Can you turn down the music? (mind)
   Would _____ down the music?

2. Can you hand in your essay first thing tomorrow? (think)
   _____ you could hand in your essay first thing tomorrow?

3. Can I come? (possible)
   Would _____ for me to come?

4. Ideally, you could help us move our things out of the house. (hoping)
   We _____ you could help us move our things out of the house.

Grammar

1a Read Articles 1 and 2 and complete the sentence.

Article 1 is _____ positive about Wikipedia _____ Article 2.

for your information . . .
We question the facts so you know the truth

1

Wikipedia has revolutionized the way encyclopedias are compiled. Its open nature has led to a democratizing process; knowledge is now not only in the hands of professors, but of the ordinary man or woman who has the interest, time, and dedication to research and document facts. No wonder the establishment feels threatened. "It's not authoritative!" they cry. "It's too left-wing!" "It doesn't represent the whole range of culture!" Of course it doesn't. It is a contemporary comment on the world. With time, today's contributors' views will be challenged and edited by a new generation.

2

Wikipedia is a valuable resource for the amateur researcher in a hurry. If you want to find out when the Crimean War started, or what *quarks* are or when Picasso painted *Guernica*, Wikipedia will tell you, with 99.99% accuracy. But for anything more complex, Wikipedia is full of potential or real misinformation. It's not the contributors' fault; they genuinely want to get it right. But, for all we know, the contributors could be five-year-olds. Wikipedia's open-source system means that anyone—young children, obsessives, and the lunatic fringe—can edit it. Because of this, no serious academic should trust Wikipedia.

next week we discuss . . .

b Correct the mistake in each sentence.

1. It is not near as complimentary about Wikipedia as the other article.

2. It suggests that Wikipedia is not nearly like as reliable as other encyclopedias.

3. It is more considerably positive about Wikipedia than the other article.

4. According to Article 2, the less we know about the contributors, less we can trust Wikipedia.

5. The author of one article is definitely not as critical of Wikipedia to the author of the other article.

6. One article implies that it's far to let everyone contribute to encyclopedias.

2a Replace the words and expressions in *italics* with words and expressions from the box. You will not use all of them.

concerning	would like
Yours sincerely	following
of your attendance	take place
a previous arrangement	be grateful
look forward to hearing	Dear
don't hesitate to contact me	

_____ **1.** We *hope to hear* from you soon.

_____ **2.** Please *get in touch* if you have any questions.

_____ **3.** *Hi*, Mrs. Dormer,

_____ **4.** Technics Solutions *wants* to invite you to our annual investors' meeting

_____ **5.** inform us *whether you will be able to come* by June 14.

_____ **6.** which will *be* at The Atrium on Rose Street at 5:00 on July 6.

_____ **7.** We would *like it* if you could

_____ **8.** *Best wishes*,

b Number the sentences in the correct order to make a formal letter.

Reading

3a Read the articles. Which community did each website target?

_____ **a.** Fashionable people   _____ **c.** Readers

_____ **b.** People who have things to sell

1

Pierre Omidyar, the son of French-Iranian immigrants, was already a millionaire before launching eBay. Omidyar's electronics site, e-shop, was bought out by Microsoft in 1996, making him a millionaire before he'd turned 30. With this money, he set up an online auction company that allowed people to show items they wished to sell; other users then made a bid. Omidyar wanted to name the site Echo Bay Technology Group. This name was already owned by a Canadian mining company, so he shortened the name to eBay®, and a legend was born. Almost immediately, eBay made a profit. The site sold goods ranging from computers to posters to underwear. The growth of eBay was phenomenal. It is now the world's most successful online business, and its users consider themselves part of a distinct community. Over 150 million registered users buy and sell goods worth $1,050 every second. The website is used by big companies such as Vodaphone and IBM to sell off excess stock, but the majority of goods still sell for less than $50.

2

It was the early 90s, the Internet boom was just beginning, and Jeff Bezos wanted to be a part of this brave, new, forward-thinking community. After leaving his job on Wall Street, Bezos decided to set up an online bookselling business. Using his garage in Seattle as an office, Bezos created Amazon.com. The idea was to make the buying of books cheap and easy, with more choices than the traditional bookstore could provide. The site had a number of features that made it attractive to potential users: fast service, search capabilities, low costs for users, tools for comparing prices of books, and personalization in the form of customer-written book reviews. As a 24-hour virtual bookstore, Amazon was convenient, cheap, and reliable. Gradually, through word-of-mouth, the company grew in popularity. Bezos had originally handled customer orders himself, but he soon realized that the company was growing too fast for one man. By 1998, the net sales were $540 million, and a whole generation of book buyers was hooked.

3

Ernst Malmsten, an events organizer, and Kajsa Leander, a supermodel, grew up in Lund, Sweden. In the late 90s, they decided to launch boo.com, a website that would create a global fashion community by selling designer clothes all over the world.

From the beginning, there were difficulties. Clothing companies didn't trust the Internet and were reluctant to sell online. Also, no one was sure that people would buy clothes without trying them on first. On November 3,1999, the day boo.com was launched, the website had 25,000 hits, but these resulted in only eight actual orders for clothes. Worse, a well-known journalist wrote a negative article about boo.com, explaining how it had taken him 81 minutes to order a product. Other problems included viruses and a fraud detection system that rejected customers' orders. By March 2000, half of boo.com's workforce had lost their jobs. While most Internet start-ups are run from garages or bedrooms, boo.com had luxurious offices in six of the world's most glamorous and expensive cities. Fresh fruit and flowers were delivered daily. Malmsten and Leander, who always traveled first-class, claimed that companies in the fashion industry needed this image. But boo.com was spending faster than it was earning, and the company was doomed.

b Are these statements true about Amazon, eBay, or boo.com?

1. The founder originally wanted a different name for the website. _____

2. The company had a high-class, stylish image. _____

3. Users of the site could post their own opinions of the things being sold. _____

4. The site sold a range of goods from the beginning. _____

5. The type of item for sale wasn't ideal for online shopping. _____

6. The founder or founders originally ran the website alone. _____

7. The founder or founders was or were already rich before launching the website. _____

8. The company had some technical problems. _____

c Find words in the articles that mean:

1. offer of a price for something (_v., n._) (Article 1) _____

2. extraordinary or remarkable (_adj._) (Article 1) _____

3. a store of goods ready for sale (_n._) (Article 1) _____

4. unwilling or not wanting to do something (_adj._) (Article 3) _____

5. new company (especially Internet companies) (_n._) (Article 3) _____

6. extremely comfortable and expensive (_adj._) (Article 3) _____

7. destined to end badly (_adj._) (Article 3) _____

Reading

1a Read about three different communities. What positive aspects of each community are described?

Positive aspects:

Community 1 _____

_____

Community 2 _____

_____

Community 3 _____

_____

Community 1

People might think that because our community is poor, the people are unhappy, or maybe there's nothing to do. But that's really not the case at all. All kinds of things go on within the townships; each one is really a real hive of activity. For example, one of the ways we entertain ourselves is through music. Music brings people together, and of course it's free. There are so many choirs here I've lost count, and they don't just sing our traditional songs; they do all sorts of other things like pop and classical music. A visitor once left us a tape of Robbie Williams, and we learned the songs and sing the harmonies. Another activity that's important here is soccer. Again, the beauty of it is that it's free and anyone can play. The girls have a team, and there's an over-60s team. The field where we play used to be covered with broken glass and had animals grazing, but we fixed it, and now it's very good. And whenever Bafana Bafana plays, we all sit around one television and cheer and sing. So, life in a township is hard, of course, but we have a way of making the best out of the things we have. No one sits around feeling sorry for himself.

Community 2

My grandfather once told me a saying. He said that the land doesn't belong to the people; the people belong to the land. I think this idea is one of the reasons why Vanuatu is special. The people are close to nature, and the nature here really is wonderful. Vanuatu is made up of lots of small islands, and we have beautiful coastlines and rainforests. The land is so fertile that we grow most of our own food, and this means that even the many poor people here won't starve. We are a close-knit community. People tend to help each other perhaps more than in built-up, developed communities. I remember a few years ago an American was stranded on one of the islands with his ten-year-old son because of a problem with the airline. I think he was a researcher. There were no stores or hotels, but the people here fed them and looked after them for three weeks until they could fly out. This is quite normal in Vanuatu. We are a spiritual people, and not very materialistic. We enjoy what we have and don't really seek material things. I hope that is how the world sees us, although I'm told that we are more famous for inventing bungee jumping!

Community 3

We were fed up with the "annoyances" of living in a regular community, so we decided to set up our own. Four years ago a group of 28 of us, all retired and all over 65, bought up some real estate and had the whole community designed and laid out for us. And this is the result. We have nothing at all against young people. In fact, most of us have children and grandchildren. But we just wanted a quiet neighborhood without noise and trash, and it works incredibly well. We are all old friends, and we have complementary skills. Jack down the road knows how to fix a car, and I used to work in real-estate law, so I deal with those issues. Reuben Barrios next door was a gardener, so he tells everyone how to grow flowers. It's everything we wanted for our old age. Our grandchildren visit us on the weekends, and we have a lot of fun, but come Monday, they're gone, and it's back to a quiet life.

b Mark the statements true (*T*) or false (*F*).

Community 1

_____ 1. The writer is from a rich area.

_____ 2. The hobbies there don't cost anything.

_____ 3. The people of the community are probably close and do many things together.

Community 2

_____ 4. Vanuatu is a place of natural beauty.

_____ 5. Most of the people of Vanuatu are wealthy.

_____ 6. The writer thinks that the people of Vanuatu are becoming more materialistic.

Community 3

_____ 7. The writer probably likes loud music.

_____ 8. The community is made up of friends.

_____ 9. The writer wishes there were more young people in the community.

c Choose the best definition.

Community 1

1. a real hive of activity
   a. full of action and productivity
   b. a place where people meet
   c. an appropriate time to do something

2. Bafana Bafana
   a. an African game
   b. a soccer team
   c. a type of music

Community 2

3. fertile
   a. beautiful and full of color
   b. free for everyone to use
   c. good for growing plants and food

4. stranded
   a. very hungry
   b. in trouble with the police
   c. couldn't get out

Community 3

5. real estate
   a. a very large house
   b. a plan made by an architect
   c. property such as houses or land

6. complementary
   a. saying how good something is
   b. the best
   c. (things) go well together, though they are different

Vocabulary

2 Complete the article with words from the box.

> unspoiled   diverse   tranquil   views
> magnificent   run-down   packed   vast
> off the beaten track

www.travelblogs.com/jilland

Traveling Sisters: The Travel Blog of Rachel and Gina

Days 12 and 13: Chiang Mai, Thailand

Greetings from Chiang Mai! Gina and I arrived early Saturday evening, which was perfect timing. Our hotel was very clean and modern, unlike the _____ (1.) place we stayed at in Bangkok! The clerk recommended that we visit the nearby Saturday Walking Street. This market is _____ (2.) and far from other sites. It wasn't very _____ (3.), probably because few tourists know about it. The vendors had a _____ (4.) array of items. There were locally produced silks, in a rainbow of _____ (5.) colors. The quality was amazing, and after a little bargaining, so were the prices. I bought a gorgeous blue and green scarf. We also saw some incredible woodcarvings, a specialty in Chiang Mai.

It just so happened that we had arrived during the Loi Krathong festival, an event that happens each November. After strolling through the market, we bought two *krathongs*, small cups made with banana leaves and lotus flowers. People put coins or hair in them. At night, they light candles on the krathongs and float them down waterways. The cups carry away bad luck. People also light paper lanterns, which float into the _____ (6.) night sky. Gina and I stood with the locals and watched. As I gazed at the lights, I just knew it was one of the most stunning _____ (7.) I had ever seen!

The next morning, Gina and I explored the Old City, an area of town _____ (8.) by modern architecture. Surrounded by ancient walls and a moat, the Old City is home to many *wats*, or temples. We stepped out of the noisy city streets and into the quiet of these _____ (9.) spaces. We even met some monks! They were very friendly and eager to practice their English. It was a great way to spend our first full day in Chiang Mai.

1 Circle the correct choice.

1. The problem with Monaco is that the *price/ cost/rate* of living is so high.

2. Buenos Aires has a *mild/calm/normal* climate. It isn't boiling in summer or freezing in winter.

3. The *health/medical/healthcare* system in Cuba used to be excellent, with many top hospitals.

4. Arguably, the highest *standard/rate/style* of living is found in Scandinavian countries.

5. For several years the crime *level/statistics/ rate* in New York has been falling.

6. Apart from the air *uncleanness/pollution/ dirt*, Mexico City is wonderful.

7. The best thing about Tokyo is its fantastic cultural *story/life/style*.

8. The *party life/night action/nightlife* in Rio de Janeiro is fantastic.

9. Hong Kong is becoming increasingly *unspoiled/diverse/varied*.

10. The best thing about Brazil is the sense of *liberty/freeing/freedom* as you walk around.

2 Add words or phrases from the box to complete the sentences. You will not use all of them.

recommend	to watch	to do	being
us to use	entering	afford	going
of watching	stand	to go	avoids
us using	to pass	urge	is
us to enter	doing		

1. I'm thinking of to Costa Rica. What's the weather like in April?

2. Dave can't to take a vacation, so he's camping in his yard this year!

3. Can you imagine an astronaut? You could go into space!

4. Mario's so lazy: he always doing the dishes.

5. I tried to persuade Gail a DVD tonight, but she didn't want to.

6. I can't smoking; cigarette smoke makes me sick.

7. They advised traveler's checks because they're safer.

8. My teachers always encouraged me my best.

9. Libby urged the competition. She was right: we won!

3 To complete the comparisons in the article, add six more words.

The online community is predicting that blogs will soon replace print journalism. While publishing material on the web is far easier ⌄*than* getting it into print, I have my doubts about this prediction. First, blogs are considerably reliable than print journalism. There are checks and balances for print journalists, and newspapers are far likely than websites to be prosecuted if they get the facts wrong. Reading a blog is almost the same reading a diary; if it is full of lies and exaggeration, there's not a lot you can do. The advantage of blogs is that they are personal and usually unedited. But more we rely on them for news, the less sure we can be that we are getting the full story. Basically, they act as a voice that cannot be silenced. The easier the web becomes to use, more diverse voices it will contain, and that's a great thing. As for me, I'm far comfortable getting my news from a newspaper!

4 Put the letters in parentheses in the correct order to complete the article.

The town where I grew up used to be a beautiful, _____ (**1.** usnpilode) little place. It was a _____ (**2.** ntrauiql), sleepy kind of town, and that's how I liked it. It was _____ (**3.** fof hte eabtne rtakc), surrounded by rolling hills and a _____ (**4.** nimaficnget) forest. I went back recently and was surprised at how much it had changed. For one thing, a new shopping mall had been built right near the center of town. I went inside, and it was _____ (**5.** apkdec) with shoppers. Then I drove to my old school, which was still _____ (**6.** gutibsln) with children, though the building looked a little _____ (**7.** nru-nwod). I went in, hoping to see some of my old teachers, but a security guard promptly kicked me out. So I drove toward the forest, assuming that some things would remain unchanged. Unfortunately, the forest didn't exist any more; they'd built a _____ (**8.** asvt) apartment complex there.

5 Do the pairs of sentences have similar (*S*) or different (*D*) meanings?

____ **1. a.** It's almost the same price whether you buy your ticket on the Internet or at the station.

    b. Buying the ticket on the Internet is a little bit cheaper, but there's hardly any difference.

____ **2. a.** I'd rather live in a quiet community than one with lots of nightlife.

    b. In my view, the more nightlife, the better.

____ **3. a.** The less we mix with that community, the less trouble we'll have.

    b. We're much better off mixing with that community.

____ **4. a.** Togo is not nearly as expensive as South Africa.

    b. South Africa is considerably more expensive than Togo.

____ **5. a.** Lugano is a little prettier than my home town.

    b. My home town isn't quite as pretty as Lugano.

____ **6. a.** Busan is not nearly as exciting as the town where I grew up.

    b. Busan is far more exciting than the town where I grew up.

6 Complete the crossword.

Across

3. I ____ you to visit the Vatican Museum while in Rome. You shouldn't miss it.

5. If you go to Panama City, ____ out for pickpockets.

8. Everyone said the movie was great, but I thought it was a little ____.

Down

1. The drinks are ____ in this nightclub. They shouldn't be this expensive!

2. You can't miss the Picasso exhibition! It's a ____.

4. The restaurant is not fancy, but its food is tasty and you get a great ____ for the money.

6. That statue isn't all it's ____ up to be. I thought it would be much more beautiful than it is.

7. You should watch ____ for the mosquitoes. There are a lot of them at this time of year.

Reading

1a Read the title of the article. What do you think the article will be about? Circle your choice.

    a. Some communities claim they have a secret way to stay young and healthy. The article describes how they manage to do it.

    b. Some communities claim that many of their people live until they are over a hundred. The article disputes these claims.

    c. Some researchers believe that ancient communities are healthier than modern societies. The article lists the problems of modern living.

b Read the article to check your answer.

c Read the article again. On a separate sheet of paper, write questions for these answers.

    1. It was an academic paper about the people he studied.

    2. A local man whose stated age changed by eleven years in only four years.

    3. It was lost when a church caught fire.

    4. Because in these societies, the older you are, the more respected you are.

    5. The condition of the people's bones, and official documents.

    6. Because they were afraid of being caught.

The old age hoax

A little old man walks the fields of Vilcabamba, Ecuador. His skin is wrinkled from exposure to the sun, and his legs move slowly, steadily. As the sky turns red, he puts down his ancient tools and walks across the valley to the mud hut that he calls
5 home. He is 140 years old.

Hard to believe? Well, Methuselah lived to be 969, according to the Bible. And, according to some, there are communities – the people of Vilcabamba, the Abkhazians of Georgia, the Hunza of Pakistan – that contain large numbers
10 of centenarians, those lucky people who live to be 100.

Let's take a trip back in time. January, 1973. Dr. Alexander Leaf, of Harvard University, publishes a report in *National Geographic* magazine that describes his journeys to study the Hunza, Abkhazians, and the Vilcabambas. He calls his report
15 *Every Day Over 100 is a Gift.* According to Leaf, there are ten times the number of centenarians found in these areas than is normal in modern Western civilizations. The article causes a minor stir in anthropology circles and one or two commercial ones too: an American entrepreneur makes plans to invest
20 in bottled water from Vilcabamba, and a Japanese company discusses building a hotel there for elderly tourists.

But then, as further studies followed Leaf's, the evidence began to point not to mythical communities with ancient youth-preserving lifestyles, but rather to lies, exaggeration, and the
25 creation of a sensational myth. Although Leaf's report sounded plausible enough at first, a number of questions arose later. When Dr. Leaf returned to Vilcabamba four years after his first visit, one of the villagers, Miguel Carpiro, had miraculously become eleven years older. Leaf asked to see Carpiro's birth certificate, but was
30 told that it had been destroyed in a church fire.

Indeed, birth records were one of the main problems; societies with low levels of literacy usually don't have them. And, in Vilcabamba, names were used repeatedly within the family, so
35 that grandfathers, fathers, and sons might have exactly the same name, adding to the confusion. Furthermore, old age is revered in societies such as Abkhazian, and so people exaggerate to improve their social status. When the exaggeration also brings
40 about increased attention and tourism, there is even further temptation to add a few years to your age.

After Leaf's report, two researchers, Mazess and Forman, went to Vilcabamba and checked skeletal conditions, as well as existing records. They found enormous inaccuracies
45 everywhere. Miguel Carpiro, who had claimed to be 121, was actually 87. His mother was born five years after he'd claimed to be born! Another researcher, a Russian geneticist named Zhores Medvedev, studied the people of Abkhazia, who had also claimed to have many centenarians. He discovered that
50 many of them had assumed the identities of their parents. Some of these people were World War I deserters, and they had used their dead parents' names in order to avoid detection.

So, myth or reality? We don't know for sure. Roger Maupin, an anthropologist, says of these people: "Their lifestyle is
55 certainly healthy. They have constant steady work, a good diet, and a small community untroubled by such things as war, technology, and the stresses these bring. But we just have no reliable evidence about their real age. Ultimately, I don't think it matters. It's not the age you live to; it's the quality of your
60 life that counts."

d Underline words or phrases in the article that mean:

1. people who are still alive at 100 (*n.*) (line 10)
2. attract a lot of attention (*v.*) (lines 17–18)
3. believable (*adj.*) (line 26)
4. deeply respected (*adj.*) (line 37)
5. importance (how much a person is respected) within a community (*n.*) (line 39)
6. causes (*v.*) (lines 39–40)
7. soldiers who run away from battle (*n.*) (line 51)
8. being found (*v.*) (line 52)

Grammar

2 Complete each sentence using the correct form of the verb in parentheses.

1. Who _____ to on the phone when I came home? (talk)
2. We could tell from his filthy clothes that he _____ in the garden for hours. (work)
3. I knew something was wrong because the dog _____ constantly. (bark)
4. Once I _____ her, I knew she was the girl for me. (meet)
5. The maid obviously hadn't come because my room _____. (clean)
6. _____ of him before you saw the movie? (hear)
7. Later, I realized that we _____ about different people! (talk)
8. I couldn't pick him up because my car _____. (fix)

3 Circle the sentence that describes each picture.

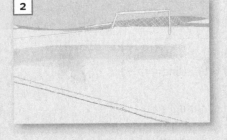

1. **a.** At midnight, when we got back, she had already put the baby to bed.
   b. At midnight, when we got back, she was putting the baby to bed.

2. **a.** The game was canceled because it had been snowing.
   b. The game was canceled because it was snowing.

3. **a.** Jim had painted the bathroom.
   b. Jim had been painting the bathroom.

4. **a.** I got home and discovered that my apartment had been broken into.
   b. I got home and discovered that my apartment was being broken into.

5. **a.** Junichi told us he had been training for the Olympics.
   b. Junichi told us he was training for the Olympics.

6. **a.** When I saw Joan, she was going to the salon.
   b. When I saw Joan, she had been to the salon.

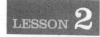

Reading

1a Read the short story on the right. Answer the questions on a separate sheet of paper.

1. Who do you think had the idea to go birdwatching?

2. What type of town do Thomas and Rosie live in?

3. Is Thomas good at spelling? How do we know?

4. What type of person is Rosie? How do we know?

5. What does the father think of Thomas's description of the birdwatching trip?

6. Why was Rosie "disgraced"?

7. How does the father feel about his children?

8. Which of these words would you use to describe the story? Circle one or more words.

   surprising   *surreal*   *traditional*
   shocking   *funny*

b Find words in the story that mean:

1. ready and waiting (*adj.*) (line 9) _____

2. high-pitched shout (*n.*) (line 20) _____

3. walking with short steps, body moving from side to side (*v.*) (line 32) _____

4. walking vigorously (usually through something) (*v.*) (line 34) _____

5. preserved in some kind of (solid) form, but no longer living, growing, or used (*adj.*) (line 35) _____

6. thrown away or abandoned (*adj.*) (line 41) _____

7. made something uneven or messy by rubbing it (*v.*) (line 42) _____

8. looking at something, angrily (*v.*) (line 48) _____

c Find the object or person in the story that these words refer to.

1. it (line 4) _____
2. on which (line 10) _____
3. this same sound (line 25) _____
4. it (line 27) _____
5. It (line 30) _____
6. it (line 33) _____
7. he (line 46) _____
8. its (line 48) _____

Birdwatcher

At 2:32 on the afternoon of July 10, eight-year-old Thomas Smith saw a large yellow-beaked eagle rise from the roof of the local post office. His sister, ten-year-old Rosie, didn't see it because she was busy
5 applying her mother's lipstick to her small, but very pretty, mouth, and in any case, she wasn't all that excited about birdwatching.

"Rosie," said Thomas. "How do you spell eagle?" His pencil was poised above a notebook that had a
10 picture of an owl on the front and on which Thomas had written "BuRds". B-u-r-d-s.

"Eagle?" said Rosie. "I-d-i-o-t."

"Very funny."

"E-e-g-l-e."
15 Thomas wrote it down. Eegle. 2:32, July 10. Franklin Road Post Office.

They crossed the street, slipping between the fat cars all stopped still in the summer heat, fingers tapping outside windows. It was at this point that
20 Thomas heard the distant shriek of seagulls and recognized the sound at once. The previous summer, they had spent a week with their parents at a beach town eating huge sausages in pools of grease and getting red-faced in the sun, and had been woken
25 every morning by this same sound.

"Rosie, how do you spell seagull?"

"Same as eagle, but it starts with an s."

At 2:58, Thomas and Rosie paused for a minute while Rosie searched her purse for the blue eye shadow
30 that she had removed from her mother's drawer. It was called Aquamarine Dream. At this moment, Thomas noticed a penguin waddling down Main Street. Thomas watched it go by, the penguin merrily traipsing through the cigarette butts and chewing gum
35 stains fossilized on the sidewalk, and Thomas wrote "Pen Win" in his notebook.

Later, while the disgraced Rosie was grounded in her room, her mother's makeup returned, Thomas sat at his father's feet and explained about the eagle on the
40 post office roof, the ostrich outside the library, and the vulture in Rosemary Gardens snacking on a discarded bag of popcorn. His father ruffled the boy's hair, laughed to himself, and thought about the wonders of the child's imagination. And the man felt at peace with
45 the world and with his two naughty children, at least until 3:11 A.M. the following morning, when he was woken by an enormous white swan sitting at the end of his bed, its yellow eyes glaring.

Vocabulary

2 Complete the book review using words from the box.

> one-dimensional   hooked   turner   base
> best-seller   gripping   down   true
> bookworm   depicts   found   avid

Meredith Johnson's new book, *Feather Man*, like her four previous novels, is a page-_____ (1.) and destined to be a _____ (2.). Unusually for Johnson, she doesn't _____ (3.) her plot on a true story (her last book was based on the _____ (4.) story of a failed bank robbery), though once again she brilliantly _____ (5.) Edinburgh's criminal underworld, where a wrong word can earn you a slashing with a razor blade, and a wrong move can get you injected with something even worse.

    She soon has the reader _____ (6.). The hero, Paul Schroeder, detective and _____ (7.), who spends half his life in a library, finds himself investigating a writer called Max Dowling, when Schroeder realizes that Dowling leaves clues to unsolved crimes in his books.

    I _____ (8.) the story totally _____ (9.), and if the characters are a little _____ (10.) — for example, an unrealistic group of criminals all seem to wear leather jackets, smoke a lot, and have frightening pets—the pace and action more than make up for it. Frankly, I couldn't put *Feather Man* _____ (11.). I recommend it highly, not only for _____ (12.) readers of Johnson's work, but for new converts, too.

3 Read what these people say about their partners. Circle the correct choice.

1. She comes *across/over/around* as very kind and gentle when you first meet her.
2. Once you *become to know/get to know/seem to know* her, you realize she's really funny.
3. The thing that *strikes/hits you/strikes you* about Tyler is that he's so intelligent.
4. What I really *think about/like for/like about* Karen is her sense of humor.
5. Matthew is *such a/so/a such* talented guy that you have to admire him.
6. He can be *a bit of/a bit/bit* mean sometimes, especially when he's in a bad mood.

4a Match the beginning of each compound adjective with its end.

____ 1. single-   **a.** minded
____ 2. self-   **b.** minded
____ 3. thick-   **c.** offish
____ 4. kind-   **d.** oriented
____ 5. stand-   **e.** hearted
____ 6. career-   **f.** skinned
____ 7. level-   **g.** sufficient
____ 8. absent-   **h.** headed

b Match the compound adjectives in Exercise 4a to the people in these paragraphs. You may match more than one to each person. Two compound adjectives are not used.

1. Bradbury was determined to claw his way to the top of the company, trampling on whoever got in his way. He had been in the business only six months when he decided that the quickest way to get promoted would be to murder William DeFries.

   _____

2. Delilah sat in the corner for the whole party. Whenever a young man approached, she immediately feigned boredom and continued sipping from her slim glass of ice-water, eyes raised to the ceiling.

   _____

3. My mother was the type of person who regularly left home in her slippers. She frequently forgot to turn off ovens, lights, televisions, and radios. She was known to make phone calls and, on being answered, immediately forget not only why she was calling, but who she was calling.

   _____

4. Being short, skinny, and ugly, I have been called names since I was old enough to walk. "Stick insect, creepy-crawly, witch, rat-face, alien, ET, lizard." I answer the name-callers with a wink and a smile. You see, I just don't care.

   _____

5. Mr. Trimble had watery gray eyes and a pocket permanently stuffed full of sweets for any children he came across. He walked with the slowness of a snail, leaving no slime, but a trail of happiness wherever he went.

   _____

Reading

1a Read three jokes and match the pictures to the jokes.

____ **1. Liar, Liar**

A policeman stops a car because it is speeding. He asks the driver for his license. "I don't have one," says the driver. "And the car's not mine. I stole it. But I think I saw a driver's license in the glove box when I put my gun in there."

"You stole it?! You have a gun in the glove box?!"

"Yes," says the driver. "I put it there just before I threw the car owner's body in the trunk." The policeman calls for backup, and five minutes later, four police cars arrive. The captain says, "Sir, may I see your license?"

"Sure," says the driver. He opens the glove box slowly and gives him the license. The police captain says, "So, no gun in the glove box?"

"Gun? Of course not!"

"And no body in the trunk?"

"What?!" says the driver. And the captain says: "My police officer told me you had a gun in the glove box and a body in the trunk."

"Yeah, and I bet the liar told you I was speeding too."

____ **2. The Cat Who Came Back**

A couple owned a cat, but the man hated it. So one day he decided to get rid of it. He drove ten blocks and threw the cat out of the car window. But when he got home, there the cat was, lying on the doormat. So the next day, he drove twenty blocks and threw the cat into a river. But, on entering his driveway, the cat was there again, fast asleep by the door.

So the next day he drove fifteen blocks, took a left, took a right, went down the highway, crossed a couple of bridges, and threw the cat into a large hole in the ground. After driving a while, he called his wife. "Is the cat there?" he asked.

"Yes," she said. "Why do you ask?"

"OK, put the cat on the phone. I'm lost and I need directions home."

____ **3. Some Good Advice**

A new manager walks into his office and finds four numbered envelopes on the desk. Number one says "Open me first." So he opens it, and finds a letter from the previous manager. It says, "When the company is having problems and you don't know what to do, open these envelopes in order." So he puts the envelopes away and forgets about them. Six months later, the company is in big trouble and the manager may lose his job. Suddenly, he remembers the envelopes, so he opens the second envelope. In it there is a message that says, "Blame everything on me, the previous manager." He does this and saves his job, and the company recovers. But, six months after this, the company is in trouble again and losing money fast. He opens the third envelope and reads the message. It says, "Blame everything on the government." He does this, and everyone agrees, and he keeps his job. Six months later, the company is in even bigger trouble, and the workers are on strike. So he opens the fourth envelope. The message says: "Prepare four envelopes."

b Complete the sentences.

Joke 1

1. The driver was stopped because he was

   _____ .

2. There wasn't a gun in the _____ or a body in the _____ .

Joke 2

3. A man wanted to _____ of a cat.

4. The man needed _____ to get home.

Joke 3

5. The second note said, "_____ everything on me."

6. The manager's final problem was that the workers were on _____ .

c Read the sentences below. Mark the sentences that are probably sarcastic (*SA*), show surprise (*S*), and those that are said calmly (*C*).

____ 1. "You stole it?! You have a gun in the glove box?!"

____ 2. "I put it there just before I threw the car owner's body into the trunk."

____ 3. "Sir, may I see your license?"

____ 4. "So, no gun in the glove box?"

____ 5. "Gun? Of course not!"

____ 6. "My police officer told me you had a gun in the glove box and a body in the trunk."

____ 7. "Yeah, and I bet the liar told you I was speeding, too."

Grammar

2 Complete each story with the participle or gerund of verbs from the box.

> have/catch   ask   play
> celebrate   call   cheat

> have/place   tell   involve
> have/make   bet   know

In the wild old days of cowboys and saloons, _____ (**1.**) at cards was likely to get you killed. _____ (**2.**) cheating in a saloon in 1857, Donald Blewett was shot dead. The men _____ (**3.**) still wanted to finish their game, however, and they needed another player, so they asked a stranger to join them. This stranger then proceeded to win over $4,000. _____ (**4.**) to the scene a while later, the police decided to try and find Donald Blewett's nearest relative. After _____ (**5.**) around to find out the dead man's name, they discovered that the stranger _____ (**6.**) his $4,000 jackpot was Blewett's son, who hadn't seen his father for over ten years.

_____ (**7.**) should never have been easier. _____ (**8.**) elaborate plans to cheat, horse owner and politician Horatio Ortiz placed "the perfect bet" on a horse race in Argentina. He owned all six of the horses _____ (**9.**) in the race, and he employed the six English jockeys. After _____ (**10.**) the jockeys the order in which they should finish, Ortiz thought he couldn't lose. However, _____ (**11.**) his bet, he got a surprise. Halfway through the race, a thick fog descended on the course. As a result, the race was declared null and void, with no winner. Ortiz, _____ (**12.**) for his money-making ability, lost a fortune.

3 Six of these sentences contain mistakes. Check the correct sentences. Correct the mistakes in the others.

____ **1.** Not having heard the music, I can't really judge it.

____ **2.** On been arrested by the police, Teresa admitted that she was guilty of fraud.

____ **3.** She broke her leg while to play hockey.

____ **4.** He stood there in front of us, desolate, robbed of everything he'd ever owned.

____ **5.** To help other people wasn't something that usually made Mrs. Davies happy.

____ **6.** Having been given the car just the day before, Lucas promptly crashed it.

____ **7.** All of the boys, hoped to be basketball stars, trained for six hours every day.

____ **8.** Told by his teacher that he had the ability to pass his exam, Kenzo finally achieved his goal.

____ **9.** Having wake up at 4:00 A.M., we were exhausted by 11:00.

____ **10.** After being listening to the speech for four hours, Bianca eventually fell asleep.

Vocabulary

4 Complete the crossword.

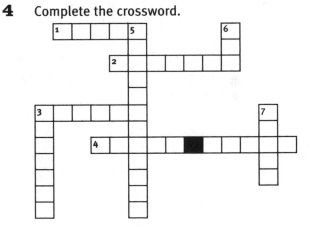

Across

1. comic drama using unlikely situations and people acting stupidly

2. a funny drawing

3. make something or someone seem ridiculous (often in order to laugh at people who have power)

4. comic moments connected to very serious subjects

Down

3. humor based on extremely strange connections

5. giving the impression that something is greater or larger than it really is

6. humorous use of words that sound the same but have different meanings

7. when you say the opposite of what you mean, for a humorous effect

1 Complete the crossword.

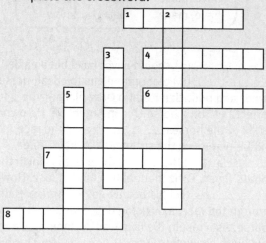

Across

1. A person who forgets little things is ____-minded.
4. A person who is difficult to talk to and not very friendly is stand-____.
6. A person who is determined to do something is single-____.
7. A person who is always thinking about how to get further in his or her career is career-____.
8. A person who is very calm, even when in a tricky situation, is level-____.

Down

2. A person who can look after himself without help is self-____.
3. A person who doesn't get offended easily when criticized is thick-____.
5. A person who is generous and nice to others is kind-____.

2 Circle the correct word or phrase.

1. In order to avoid hurting people, I think it's OK to tell ____.
   a. a feeble excuse   b. a white lie   c. a rumor
2. Advertising writers aren't exactly liars, but they tend to slightly ____.
   a. exaggerate   b. gossip   c. tell lies
3. We heard the fire alarm, but it turned out to be a ____.
   a. rumor   b. false   c. hoax
4. My mother is the best ____ I know.
   a. bookworm   b. storyteller   c. story
5. Are you good at telling ____?
   a. storytellers   b. jokes   c. hoaxes

3 Complete the sentences using the correct form of verbs from the box.

memorize	drive	face
turn into	write	make
get up	leave	read

1. By midday I was really tired, because I _____ on the freeway since 5 A.M.

2. She said all the noise was because the building next door _____ a shopping mall. The work wouldn't be completed until the following May.
3. They desperately wanted to see Francesca, but the janitor told them that she _____ already.
4. One of the children recited the whole story. Apparently, he _____ it for weeks.
5. When I got home, the fridge _____ a weird noise, so I called the repairman.
6. He _____ his autobiography in the months before he died, so although it wasn't finished, we had a good idea of his life story.
7. My friends knew the movie had a twist in the end, but I didn't because I _____ the book.
8. Rob tried to take a photo of Lily, but she _____ the wrong way.
9. _____ you _____ early this morning? I thought I heard you.

4 Correct the sentences by adding or crossing out one word.

1. You're such fast swimmer; I could never keep up with you.
2. What one thing I don't like about Samantha is that she's so selfish.
3. The thing strikes you about Tami is her determination.
4. He can be a bit of annoying sometimes, but his heart's in the right place.
5. Once you get to know of Maurice, you'll like him.

5 Circle the correct choice. More than one answer may be possible.

1. *To hope/Hoping/Hoped* to find a new wife, James settled in San Francisco.
2. *Restored/Having been restored/After restored* to its former glory, the painting was re-hung.
3. *Ran/To run/Running* marathons is what she does best.
4. I know the man *having sat/sat/sitting* in the blue car.
5. *While driving/Driven/Having driven* in the tunnel, keep your lights on.
6. *On hearing/Heard/Having heard* the news, he rushed over to the hospital.
7. *Buried/Being buried/Burying* in the cemetery is a famous scientist of the early twentieth century.
8. *After catching/After being caught/Having been caught*, the robber put down his gun.
9. The photos *taken/being taken/having been taken* today will turn out fine. The light is perfect.
10. *After being treated/Treating/Treated* by experts, the dog began to recover.

6 Match the descriptions to types of humor from the box. Two are not used.

black humor	cartoons	farce
surreal humor	irony	puns
exaggeration	satire	

1. Comedian John Weeding spent an hour of his great show doing impressions of President Obama and other politicians, and the audience lapped up his hilarious take on modern society. _____

2. We see the usual tricks of the genre in this tedious play: mistresses hiding in wardrobes, husbands caught with their pants down, and a plot that goes from the silly to the ridiculous. _____

3. Why is a bad joke like a broken pencil? It has no point. If you like this type of humor—and most children do—*The Bumper Book of Kids' Jokes* is for you. _____

4. He goes way beyond what you usually find in the back pages of the newspaper. The writing and drawing are so exquisite that he's been called a mix between Leonardo and Woody Allen. _____

5. Her whole act is based on creating bizarre combinations. At one point, she compares a chocolate cake to the history of space flight, and after the intermission she emerges wearing a lobster on her head. _____

6. The entire play revolves around a search for a dead body. Somehow, Luke Williams manages to wring humor out of a very dark situation. _____

Moving forward

Vocabulary

1a Match the words to their common collocations.

____ 1. serious	a. gravity
____ 2. special	b. technology
____ 3. foreseeable	c. injury
____ 4. computer	d. future
____ 5. genetic	e. engineering
____ 6. latest	f. nerd
____ 7. defy	g. power

b Complete the sentences with collocations from Exercise 1a.

1. If your laptop is broken, talk to John. He's such a _____ that it'll be easy for him to fix.

2. She likes to have all the _____. Her electronic devices are never out of date.

3. In the future, scientists may be able to use _____ to detect and stop diseases before they become harmful.

4. In the _____, all cars may be controlled by computer technology, rather than human drivers.

5. Although the cars were damaged in the accident, there were no _____ or deaths.

6. I think everyone dreams of being able to _____ and fly.

7. He looked like a normal man, but he had a _____: he was incredibly strong.

Reading

2 Read the article and choose the best title. ____

a. Superheroes—too strong for their own good?

b. Real-life superheroes—inspiration for developing superhero characters

c. Making a superhero—fact or fiction?

From gamma-radiation to radioactive spiders, superheroes are born in a variety of weird and wonderful ways. But how realistic are they?

Being born on other planets, or finding cosmic lanterns, requires a huge leap of the imagination. But what about the humans who develop special powers by slightly more prosaic means—how plausible are they?

Take The Incredible Hulk: Scientist Dr. Robert Banner receives a huge dose of gamma rays while working on a nuclear bomb. Gamma rays are real enough, being produced by nuclear explosions, but the bad news is that the gamma-radiation that gave Robert Banner his powers would only have caused fatal radiation sickness in real life.

Forgetting that minor point, Lois Gresh, author of *Science and Superheroes*, argues it's just about possible to create a believable version of The Hulk. Banner could take large amounts of (highly dangerous) anabolic steroids to produce that pumped-up look, which in real life could cause his notorious rages, as they increase aggressive mood swings. As for the green skin, French genetic researchers have at least created a glowing green rabbit by genetic engineering, using fluorescent protein.

Spider-Man, on the other hand, has bigger problems. While a radioactive spider could exist (spiders are tolerant to radiation), an animal does not transfer DNA via a bite. And even if it did, it couldn't fuse with our DNA. If being ingested were enough to make this happen, we'd get characteristics of, say, apples or chickens whenever we ate them.

Batman—the "Dark Knight"—might be the most realistic of the heroes, says Gresh. It is, of course, possible for a person to train obsessively in martial arts and subjects such as criminology. But in this case, it's

gadgets that make Batman who he is. Most of Batman's toys, from his tiny cameras, to smoke grenades, to superstrong ropes, exist in the 21st century. Even creating a batmobile shouldn't present modern carmakers with too much difficulty.

Grammar

3 On a separate sheet of paper, write sentences about the article using the words in parentheses.

Ex: I . . . you would find a cosmic lantern. (whether)

I doubt whether you would find a cosmic lantern.

1. Gamma rays . . . produced by nuclear explosions. (definitely)
2. It's . . . that if Dr. Banner had received this radiation, he would have died. (likely)
3. There . . . we could create a believable version of The Hulk in reality. (slight)
4. Giving him anabolic steroids would . . . create his pumped-up look. (almost)
5. These . . . cause him to become more aggressive and moody. (might)
6. There . . . that we could create green skin by genetic engineering. (remote)
7. A radioactive spider . . . exist. (conceivably)
8. An animal . . . of transferring DNA via a bite. (stands)
9. If it did transfer its DNA, it wouldn't . . . of fusing with our DNA. (chance)
10. If ingesting DNA were enough to change our own DNA, we . . . adopt the characteristics of chickens and apples when we ate them. (presumably)
11. Batman . . . be the most realistic of the heroes. (well)
12. There . . . that modern carmakers could even create a batmobile. (distinct)

4 Complete the sentences with words from the box.

conceivably	against	doubt	well
likelihood	doubtful	slight	any
possibility	chances	bound	stand

1. **A:** Do you think there's _____ chance that we'll see Martha this weekend?

   B: I wouldn't count on it, but there's a _____ chance that she'll show up.
2. The odds are _____ us meeting the sales targets for this quarter, but there's a strong _____ that things will improve over the coming months.
3. Rooney doesn't _____ a chance of being chosen for the team.
4. I _____ whether they'll finish the work by the end of the week.
5. We may _____ have the chance to explore the area in more detail later.
6. Why did you do that? It's _____ to upset her.
7. It's _____ that they could have chosen a worse time to announce the news.
8. It could _____ help us in the future.
9. There's every _____ that he will resign soon.
10. The _____ are that we'll beat them in the Cup Final.

Reading

5 Read the news story. Then answer the questions on a separate sheet of paper.

Real-life Superheroes

Leisa Hodgkinson is a small woman, but she lifted a one-ton car off a seven-year-old boy trapped underneath. The boy was severely injured but has since recovered completely and now calls Leisa "Wonder Woman." She said at the time that she found the strength to lift the car after thinking of her own son, who was the same age as the trapped boy.

Miami man Tony Santores won an award from the mayor for outstanding bravery in 2000, after helping to rescue a mother and child from a burning building in a daring climb worthy of Spider-Man. He scaled the front of the building, despite minimal hand and foot-holds, and stayed in the smoke-filled room with the two to comfort them until the fire-fighters arrived.

1. Why does the young boy call Leisa "Wonder Woman"?
2. Why did Tony Santores climb up the side of the building?

Vocabulary

1 Circle the correct word to complete each sentence.

1. What are you ____ to later? We're going out for a meal.

   a. up   **b.** in   **c.** on

2. Do you have anything ____ up for tonight?

   a. straight   **b.** going   **c.** lined

3. We *were* planning to all meet for lunch next week, but the plans have fallen ____ .

   a. off   **b.** out   **c.** through

4. Unfortunately, I'm ____ up all week figuring out the accounts.

   a. tied   **b.** turned   **c.** lined

5. Please try and come. Can't you ____ out of going to see your grandmother?

   a. go   **b.** come   **c.** get

6. They called ____ the wedding because she's changed her mind.

   a. on   **b.** of   **c.** off

7. I'll let you know if anything else comes ____ .

   a. up   **b.** on   **c.** in

8. Do you know if the meeting is still ____ ?

   a. for   **b.** on   **c.** in

2 Match the beginning of the sentence to its end.

____ 1. She's more or

____ 2. I was kind of hoping

____ 3. I only see them once in a

____ 4. We work mainly with textiles and

____ 5. We'll be arriving at

____ 6. We were sort

____ 7. We go camping from

a. while.

b. about five-ish.

c. less finished redecorating.

d. of expecting to hear from you.

e. you could help.

f. time to time.

g. that kind of thing.

Grammar

3 Circle the correct choice.

1. *I'll/I'm going to* pick you up from the airport if you want.

2. I have a doctor's appointment this afternoon, so *I'm leaving/I leave* work at 3 P.M.

3. What sort of job do you think you *will do/will be doing* in ten years?

4. By the time we get there, all the food *will be/will have been* eaten.

5. I'm sure you'll have a great time wherever *you decide/you'll decide* to go.

6. He asked if we *will/would* take this case for him.

7. The reception is bad in here. *I'll/'m going to* call you back in a minute.

8. He's not coming until Thursday, and we *'ll be finishing/'ll have finished* by then.

9. The flight *leaves/is going to leave* at 9:20.

Reading

The "Slow movement"

(1) Carl Honoré, a recovered "speedaholic," had an epiphany that caused him to slow down the hectic pace of his life. A journalist based in London, Honoré read a newspaper article on time-saving tips that referenced a book of one-minute bedtime stories. He found it an appealing idea, since he'd already developed the habit of speed-reading stories to his son. "My first reaction was, yes, one-minute bedtime stories," he said. "My next thought was, whoa, has it really come to this? That was really when a light bulb went off in my head."

(2) He realized he had become so anxious to rush through the nightly ritual that he was reading seven or even eight stories in less time than he'd normally spend reading one. He wasn't making the most of this quality time.

(3) So, he embarked on finding a way to address the issue of "time poverty," the constant fast-forward motion in which many overscheduled, stressed-out people are always rushing toward their next task—work, meals, family time—rather than savoring what they consider most important.

(4) Honoré's book, *In Praise of Slowness: How a Worldwide Movement Is Challenging the Cult of Speed*, has made him the unofficial godfather of a growing cultural shift toward slowing down. "[There's a] backlash against the mainstream dictate that faster is always better, which puts quantity always ahead of quality," he said. "People all across the West are waking up to the folly of that."

(5) For advocates of the Slow Movement, it's not about rejecting technology or changing modern life completely, but rather about keeping it all in balance—not talking on the phone, driving, and checking email while headed to the drive-thru before the next meeting.

"I love technology. I love speed. You need some things to be fast—hockey . . ., a fast Internet connection," Honoré said. "But," he said, "my passion for speed had become an addiction. I was doing everything faster."

(6) What to Do?

To make the transition to a slower life, Honoré has several suggestions: don't schedule something in every free moment of your day—prioritize activities and cut from the bottom of the list; limit television watching; and keep an eye on your "personal speedometer" so you can gauge when you are rushing for speed's sake rather than necessity.

(7) But don't expect the change to happen immediately—or even naturally. "You don't slow down by snapping your fingers, "Now I'm slow," said Honoré, who got a speeding ticket on his way to a Slow Food dinner as he researched the book. "That happens," he said. "My life has been transformed by it, but I still feel that old itch."

4a Read the article. Mark the statements true (*T*) or false (*F*).

_____ 1. Carl Honoré came to a slow realization that he was living life too fast.

_____ 2. He was reading an article about ways to spend more quality time with your children.

_____ 3. Carl initially thought that one-minute bedtime stories were a good idea, since he regularly read stories to his son.

_____ 4. He reflected that he needed to readdress the priorities in his life.

_____ 5. According to the article, people are stressed because they fail to think ahead to the next task.

_____ 6. Carl believes that people are starting to question whether quality is better than quantity.

_____ 7. People who join the Slow Movement do not use computers, travel in cars, or watch television.

_____ 8. His advice is to reduce the number of things you do by deciding what is least important.

b Underline words or phrases in the article that mean:

1. desperate (to do something) (*adj.*) (paragraph 2)
2. began (something long and difficult) (*v.*) (paragraph 3)
3. enjoying (*v.*) (paragraph 3)
4. a strong negative reaction (*adj.*) (paragraph 4)
5. to measure (*v.*) (paragraph 6)
6. a desire to do something you should not (*n.*) (paragraph 7)

c Complete the sentences using words or phrases from Exercise 4b.

1. We _____ on a long, difficult journey.
2. I'm _____ to speak to Phyllis before she leaves.
3. Try to _____ the views while you are here. We might never come back.
4. It was hard to _____ his reaction to the new ideas.
5. There has been a strong _____ to the changes.

Vocabulary

1 Complete each sentence by putting the letters in parentheses in the correct order.

1. There is a lot of pressure, and the job is very _____. (niegmdand)
2. She is a naturally _____ piano player. (fitegd)
3. The teenagers in the area are thugs in the _____. (kanimg)
4. Mozart was a musical _____. (dipogry)
5. The movie star was the subject of much _____ from his fans. (donulatai)
6. Staff members are trained by their _____. (srepe)
7. People who dye their hair strange colors used to be considered _____. (karsef)

Reading

2 Read the article. Make a list of Kishan's interests and achievements on a separate sheet of paper.

Nine-year-old calls the shots

(1) The director is barking orders from the edit suite as he cuts a shot featuring Jackie Shroff, a leading Indian movie star. It could be an everyday scene in Bollywood—except the director is a nine-year-old boy.

(2) Master Kishan, as he is known, has already been in 24 movies and appeared in more than 1,000 episodes of a popular television soap opera. He is now fulfilling another dream: becoming the youngest director not just in India, but in the world. "I am different from other children, because this is the age for children to play," admitted Kishan, sitting in his director's seat, his feet not quite touching the floor. "I like playing, but not as much as other children. I don't know if the movie will be successful. I hope it will be. I have a good feeling about it."

(3) Dressed in a black corduroy shirt and dark jeans, he looked like any other affluent middle-class Indian child. Later, at a local cafe, he ordered coffee and mysore pak, a buttery sweet pudding, while fielding approaches from admiring fans.

(4) Kishan, whose favorite actors are Arnold Schwarzenegger and Amithabh Bachchan, a Bollywood superstar, began his acting career at age four, after his friends urged his parents to send him for an audition. He was given a part in *Goddess of the Village*, a fantasy adventure, before landing a leading role in *Papa Pandu*, a daily Bangalore soap. He wrote a hit song for a movie at the age of six, and has sung on others.

(5) Kishan's father, Shri Kanth, a tax official, said his son had been obsessed with cameras since he was a toddler. "We noticed that when the camera was on him his behavior would improve," he said. "After he started working on the soap, the staff would complain that he asked too many questions about this shot and that shot."

(6) Kishan's transition to director began after he talked to children selling newspapers beside a busy road in Bangalore. When he asked them why they were not at school, some replied that they were orphans, others that they would be beaten if they went home without any money. Kishan was so moved that he wrote a short story about his encounter. "I want them to go to school, and I hope the film encourages them to want to go," he said.

(7) With the help of local journalists, he turned his story into a screenplay, *C/o Footpath*, about a Bangalore boy drugged by a woman who uses him as a prop to beg on the streets.

(8) Ironically, Kishan's commitments mean that he has attended school for only ten days a month during filming. His secretary picks up class notes to help him keep up. Kishan, nevertheless, shows little sign of missing classes. He speaks good English and Kanada, the local language, and understands Hindi and Tamil.

(9) Shri Kanth, however, worries that his son is missing childhood, and recently invited his friends to bring their children on a beach holiday, so that Kishan could play. He was surprised to see him building row after row of sand castles. "When I asked him why he was building them in rows, he held his hands up to make a frame, and said it was to give the shot depth," he said. A child psychologist friend has reassured him his son is fine.

3 Read the article again. Then answer the questions on a separate sheet of paper.

1. What makes Kishan different from other children his age?
2. How did Kishan become involved in acting?
3. What triggered Kishan's move toward becoming a director?
4. What inspired Kishan's short story?
5. What does he hope to achieve through the movie?
6. How does Kishan keep up with his school work?
7. Why does his father worry?

4 Find words or expressions in the article that mean:

1. shouting instructions (*v.*) (paragraph 1) _____

2. wealthy (*adj.*) (paragraph 3) _____
3. encouraged (*v.*) (paragraph 4) _____
4. think about something all the time (*v.*) (paragraph 5) _____
5. be hit many times (*v.*) (paragraph 6) _____
6. feel a strong emotion (sad/sympathetic) (*adj.*) (paragraph 6) _____
7. a meeting (*n.*) (paragraph 6) _____
8. something you use to help achieve a special effect (theatrical) (*n.*) (paragraph 7) _____
9. not fall behind (with work/study) (*v.*) (paragraph 8) _____
10. make someone feel calmer/less worried (*v.*) (paragraph 9) _____

Grammar

5 Circle the correct choice.

1. No sooner *we had heard/had we heard* the news, than the police called to tell us what had happened.
2. *Not only did she/Not only she did* break the rules, but she also lied about her behavior.
3. Only when *everyone has arrived/has everyone arrived* can we begin the discussions.
4. Rarely *have I been/I have been* so upset about something.
5. *Not since I went/Since I didn't go* to college have I made so many new friends.
6. No way *I am going/am I going* to pay for their mistake!

7. *Only if/If only* we work night and day will we get the job finished on time.
8. No longer *you do need to/do you need to* stand in long lines at airports. You can check in yourself!
9. Only after she left *did I/I did* realize what had happened.
10. Not only *the service is great/is the service great*, but it's the cheapest hotel in the area.

6 Complete each sentence with the correct word or phrase.

1. _____ could be more exotic than these picturesque islands.
2. _____ recently have we begun to understand how the disease spreads.
3. Not _____ the organizer called me did I find out about the meeting.
4. No _____ had the plane taken off than they had to make an emergency landing.
5. _____ for one minute did I think I would win the competition.
6. _____ will you find such fantastic examples of the style.
7. Never _____ have we achieved such great sales.
8. _____ when she began to sing did we realize she had a special talent.
9. _____ if you have your bags checked will you be allowed through the entrance.
10. _____ again will I ride on an elephant!

1 Complete the crossword.

Across

3. I'll let you know if anything ____ up.

6. She has a dental ____ this morning, so she's driving to my house this afternoon.

8. I was wondering what you were ____ to over the weekend.

11. I won't be able to go to the movies on Friday. There's an office party that night and I can't ____ out of it.

12. I have to work overtime this month, so our plans to visit Vancouver have ____ through.

Down

1. If you go to Panama City, ____ out for pickpockets.

2. Her phone has no ____ where she's at, so she'll call me back later.

4. Do you have anything ____ up for tonight?

5. We're ____ to pick her up from the airport at 9:00.

7. I can't make it tomorrow. I'm a little ____ up.

9. Are our ____ to see a movie still on?

10. We've had to ____ off the trip because we are just too busy.

2 Put the words in the correct order to make sentences.

1. winning/the/are/series/against/odds/their/the

   _____

2. the/we/flight/well/her/on/may/see

   _____

3. the/later/it/are/will/chances/that/rain

   _____

4. it/we/everything/doubtful/will/that/is/finish/today

   _____

5. competition/is/that/there/a/beat/distinct/we'll/the/possibility

   _____

6. promotion/he'll/likelihood/is/every/get/there/that/the

   _____

7. that/idea/to/well/excellent/prove/may/be/an

   _____

8. there/could/catch/a/chance/is/train/that/we/slight/the/earlier

   _____

3 Complete these sentences about the future, using the correct form of the verbs in parentheses. There may be more than one possibility.

1. That's fine. I _____ you next week to confirm the details. (call)

2. We _____ all the work by February. (finish)

3. OK, the taxi _____ to pick us up in half an hour. (come)

4. I have no idea what I _____ next year. (do)

5. Is Anna feeling OK? She looks like she _____ sick. (be)

6. Let me help you. I _____ this pile, and you deal with the rest. (take)

7. I have to leave at 5:00. I _____ Michael to discuss the budget. (meet)

8. The traffic is awful. I'm worried I _____ late. (be)

9. It was really good to see you. Hopefully, I _____ you again soon. (see)

10. I'm stuck at work and I don't know when I _____ home. (get)

4 Seven of these sentences contain mistakes. Check the correct sentences. Correct the mistakes in others.

_____ 1. Not only they apologized for the inconvenience, but they have refunded the money!

_____ 2. No sooner do you ask her to do a job than she has done it.

_____ 3. Only after did I repeatedly ask them did I manage to get a response.

_____ 4. Not since 2005 there has been such a hot summer.

_____ 5. Rarely do you find someone with such great talent.

_____ 6. Never before we have been able to photograph these small creatures in such detail.

_____ 7. Only if we keep looking we will ever find the solution.

_____ 8. No way am I going to dress up as Superman!

_____ 9. Nowhere it does say that we aren't allowed to use this room.

_____ 10. Not for one minute did I thought I would have to clean the whole place.

5 Complete the conversations.

1. **A:** How often do you manage to see your grandmother?
   B: Once in a _____.

2. **A:** How long do you think the meeting will last?
   B: Pretty _____ all day.

3. **A:** Should we get started early?
   B: OK. How about about six-_____?

4. **A:** What does your new job involve?
   B: There is a lot of talking to clients and that _____ of thing.

5. **A:** Let's split the bill.
   B: Actually, I was _____ of hoping you could pay.

6. **A:** What time shall we meet?
   B: About eight or _____.

7. **A:** How often do you go to the city?
   B: Only _____ in a while.

8. **A:** When should we meet?
   B: In an hour or _____.

9. **A:** Do you ever visit your home town?
   B: Yes. I go back every so _____.

10. **A:** Does it snow here much?
    B: _____ much all year.

Vocabulary

1 Complete the sentences by putting the letters in parentheses in the correct order.

1. He came into a _____ when his father died. (netourf)

2. It is common to _____ in the stores to bring the price down. (galgeh)

3. Those bankers make their fortunes betting on changes in the _____ market. (ctoks)

4. Let me buy everyone a drink. I got a _____ today! (saire)

5. The business is trying to attract _____ families. (ghih-monice)

6. Her ideas are unique, so her work is absolutely _____. (crisepels)

7. It doesn't affect our salary, because we're paid on _____. (smocsimino)

8. They have done really well considering their last business went _____. (knaptrub)

2 Match the beginning of each sentence to its end.

_____ 1. It was important that the brothers had a good relationship, as they were

_____ 2. They decided to buy their uncle

_____ 3. You need to strike the

_____ 4. It's time he rolled up his

_____ 5. They hired a consultant to

_____ 6. They kept their business and private affairs separate in order not to

_____ 7. I come from a marketing

_____ 8. It will be up to the new manager to execute the

a. sleeves and got on with what he has to do.

b. crunch the numbers.

c. 50-50 partners in the business.

d. jeopardize their friendship.

e. right balance between working hard and enjoying yourself.

f. strategy we decide on.

g. out of his share of the company.

h. background.

Grammar

3 On a separate sheet of paper, rewrite the sentences to increase the emphasis. Use the words in parentheses.

Ex: Inflation is making it increasingly difficult for young people to buy a home. (own)

Inflation is making it increasingly difficult for young people to buy their own home.

1. It isn't certain that giving aid is the best way to help poorer countries. (means)

2. Kandinsky abandoned his law studies in order to train as an artist in Munich. (even)

3. Marco Diacono planted the UK's first ever olive grove in 2006. He hoped that global warming would help the trees to survive. (It)

4. We went to the Pantanal, in Brazil, to enjoy the wildlife, but I got a shock when I found an eight-foot-long caiman outside my tent. (did)

5. I would suggest you stay along the coast near Amalfi. (need)

Reading

4a Read the story. Describe how it makes you feel.

_____

_____

My Missing Brother

While most people have lots of memories about their older siblings, my memories of my older brother are limited. Buck was 14 years older than me—that in itself set us apart in different generations and different worlds. Before he went to prison, I have only the <u>faded</u> memories of a young child. No matter how I try, it is difficult to recall what life was like with him before <u>incarceration</u>. I do remember riding on his shoulders at the county fair and how he showed me how to skip a stone across the river. But beyond that, my mind <u>draws a blank</u>. My strongest childhood memories are about visiting him with my parents at the <u>penitentiary</u> in Elmira, New York.

It was a long drive to get there, and when we arrived, we were never alone. Other families waited in line as the electronic prison gates opened and closed loudly behind us in a process that seemed to me to take forever. My parents had to sign in, get fingerprinted, and go through <u>a pat down</u> to make sure they weren't carrying anything in. The process made me very uncomfortable, and I would get very quiet and listen to the <u>banging</u> of metal and the echoes of voices in the cold, uninviting rooms.

They would take us to the visiting room where armed guards watched carefully as prisoners were brought in. My brother would <u>saunter</u> over with a smile on his face looking tall and handsome and in good health. He would sit on the other side of a stainless steel table, separated from us by a wire

covered fence that just allowed us to touch each others' fingers in place of a handshake, a hug, or a kiss. My mother would cry and my father would talk to my brother in quiet, low tones while my eyes <u>darted around</u> the room at the other <u>inmates</u> and their families. Finally my brother would call my name and ask me about school or comment on what I was wearing. I don't remember what we actually talked about. I <u>relished</u> his attention, though I recall I was very shy around him.

My strongest memories are about how he looked, how he smiled when he saw us, how he looked straight at me when we talked, and how his face changed when we had to say good-bye. Even today I grow sad at what I missed in not having my only brother at home with me.

b Answer the questions on a separate sheet of paper.

1. What memories does the writer have of her brother before prison?
2. Why does she remember the sound of the electronic prison gates?
3. What process took place before the girl and her parents could see her brother?
4. How did the girl react to this process?
5. What things did the girl notice about her brother during the visits?

5 Find the underlined words or phrases in the story that mean:

1. loud noise _____
2. prisoners _____
3. being in prison _____
4. be searched _____
5. prison _____
6. unclear _____
7. can't remember _____
8. walk proudly _____
9. looked quickly _____
10. enjoyed _____

Vocabulary

1 Add one word to complete each sentence.

1. We have volunteered _____ help move people out of the disaster area.

2. Since the old manager left, the office has _____ spiraled.

3. Unfortunately, the soccer player gave his wife _____ of attorney, and she spent all the money.

4. The local farmers invested in the water company but never saw a _____ of the profit that was made.

5. He was a media millionnaire, but after the scandal he _____ bankruptcy.

6. Sam hasn't been able to work since the car accident, so he's going _____ sue the other driver.

Grammar

2 Complete the sentences using the correct form of the verbs in parentheses.

1. If I _____ my car here, I _____ you a lift. (have) (offer)

2. If it _____ for Jamie, we _____ for a long time. (not be) (wait)

3. If you _____ carefully to what I said, this _____! (listen) (not happen)

4. Provided that she _____ all the medications, she _____ fine. (take) (be)

5. If only they _____ us ten minutes earlier, we _____ the order. (call) (cancel)

6. Unless Mr. Lee _____ his strategy, the business _____ bankrupt. (change) (go)

7. Should they happen _____ her the job, would she _____ it? (offer) (accept)

3 Complete the beginning of each sentence with the correct word. Then circle the correct ending.

1. _____ that the team keeps playing as they are right now,
   a. we had a good chance of winning the cup.
   b. we have a good chance of winning the cup.

2. Should you _____ to see Brad on your travels,
   a. could you tell him I've been trying to contact him?
   b. you could have told him I'd been trying to contact him.

3. If it _____ been for Selena telling us,
   a. we never realized what they were planning.
   b. we never would have realized what they were planning.

4. If you _____ like to see the rest of the house,
   a. I could have left the key, and you could show yourself around.
   b. I can leave you the key, and you can show yourself around.

5. If _____ we hadn't bought the tickets already,
   a. then we could change our plans.
   b. then we changed our plans.

6. As _____ as Sheila still works there,
   a. she should be able to give you all the information you need.
   b. she could be able to give you all the information you need.

Vocabulary

4 Complete the paragraph with words from the box.

> generosity   lavishly   vision   deal
> Foundation   inspired   impact
> admirable   dedicate   charity
> donating   fortune   mission

Warren Buffet, the world's greatest stock market investor, announced he was giving away most of his $24 billion _____ (1.). The world's second richest man is _____ (2.) the money to the Bill and Melinda Gates _____ (3.), whose _____ (4.) is to tackle AIDS and global poverty. This is _____ (5.) on an industrial scale. The _____ (6.) of these two men will now far outstrip the contribution of most aid organizations to Africa. The domino effect could have an equally significant _____ (7.): if important role-models _____ (8.) a great _____ (9.) of their wealth to helping the poor and the sick, then perhaps others might be _____ (10.) to give away money rather than simply spend it _____ (11.) on themselves and their families. Two hundred years ago, William Blake argued that charity, however _____ (12.) on an individual level, is wrong because it delays reform and perpetuates economic injustice. Doubtless, many still agree with that view. But the sheer scale of the Gates–Buffett "mega-merger," and their joint _____ (13.) for a way towards a better future, is surely bad news for critics of the market system.

Reading

5a Read the article quickly. What is the significance of these numbers?

1. 64   2. 30s   3. 2.5 million   4. 80–100   5. 30   6. $103 million

Instant millionaires need help

1 The high-tech world is making thousands of very young people very rich, but according to psychologists, it is also creating a new illness—sudden-wealth syndrome.

2 Some seek help because they are too rich and cannot handle their wealth, others because they crave more money or feel guilty. Dr. Stephen Goldbart, a psychologist, runs the Money, Meaning & Choices Institute near Silicon Valley, where 64 new millionaires are reportedly created every day. Most of them are people in their 20s and 30s who find themselves suddenly rich, a group Dr. Goldbart calls the "Siliconaires."

3 He noticed a change several years ago, when people from middle-class backgrounds started coming into large sums of money. With the dot.com trend of recent years, his client numbers have steadily increased. In April, Merrill Lynch reported that the number of millionaires in the United States and Canada has risen almost 40% since 1997, to 2.5 million.

4 Becoming unexpectedly rich has its drawbacks, Dr. Goldbart says, and there should be some amount of sympathy for those who cannot handle sudden wealth. "It can ruin their lives, rip their families apart, and lead them on a path of destructive behavior," he says. "Money does not always bring peace and fulfillment. They lose balance. Instead of money solving all their problems, it often brings guilt, stress, and confusion."

5 People who are used to working 80 to 100 hours a week on their fledgling enterprise suddenly find they no longer need to work and are able to retire at the age of 30. However, the newfound leisure puts them into a premature mid-life crisis. Some experience panic attacks, severe depression, and insomnia, Dr. Goldbart says. Others withdraw from society or go on maniacal shopping sprees.

6 Some newly rich feel guilty about having so much money and feel they are not entitled to it, or that they do not deserve it. Others become paranoid, thinking they will be exploited because of their wealth, or they become obsessed with making even more money. People most affected are the "new rich," for whom wealth was not part of their upbringing and who expected to spend their lives working. Anxiety and depression can also come from "ticker shock" as they watch the vagaries in the stock market, particularly a plunge when they have not exercised their stock options.

7 Part of Dr. Goldbart's cure for the unhappy rich is to get them involved in the community and not just writing checks to charities. British Columbia's Rory Holland, executive vice-president of Itemus, made his millions when the company he was involved in for eight years was sold for $103 million in 1998. He now devotes much of his time to four non-profit groups, serves on their boards, and helps raise money.

8 Dr. Goldbart believes he is the only psychologist, along with family counselor Joan DiFuria, providing therapy for the rich, and would like to see more colleagues provide the service. "These people [the rich] are sensitive to how people feel and are reluctant to use our kind of service," he says. "But we help them regain the balance they've lost."

b Read the article again. Answer the questions on a separate sheet of paper.

1. What has caused the increase in the number of millionaires?
2. What feelings can people who come into sudden wealth experience? How can these feelings affect them?
3. Who might be particularly affected?
4. What might be the cause of these feelings?
5. What does Dr. Goldbart suggest as a cure?
6. How does Dr. Goldbart feel the public should treat sudden millionaires?

6 Complete the sentences with words or phrases from the article.

1. I have so much work at the moment, I just can't _____ it. (paragraph 2)
2. I've given up caffeine, but I still _____ coffee first thing in the morning. (paragraph 2)
3. For me, the advantages outweigh the _____ when you're living in a city like Bogota. (paragraph 4)
4. The effect of the earthquake was literally to _____ the whole community. (paragraph 4)
5. The plans aren't very advanced yet. It's just a _____ idea. (paragraph 5)
6. He's quit his job, taken up jogging, and started dance classes. I think he's having a _____ . (paragraph 5)
7. She took all the credit for the ideas, even though she was not _____ to do so. (paragraph 6)
8. My father died when I was young, so we had a fairly difficult _____ . (paragraph 6)

Vocabulary

1 Complete the crossword.

Across

4. As a boss, he is very ____ of his employees.
5. I enjoy the ____ of working for myself.
6. The company invests in a private ____ plan on your behalf.
8. We get strange requests from our clients, so some of our tasks can be quite ____.
11. The employees received bonuses in recognition of their ____.
12. The number one ____ in this company is customer satisfaction.
13. The offices are modern and spacious, and there are lots of like-minded people, so it's a really good working ____.

Down

1. The pay is $39,000 a year, which is a good ____.
2. Abcom is a growing company, so there are plenty of ____ for promotion.
3. One of the best things about working here is the ____ of the location.
7. Most of the workers enjoyed a high degree of job ____.
9. We attend conferences and workshops as part of our professional ____.
10. It's a great job if you have children because of the ____ working hours.
12. Anyone can ____ an idea for improving the business.

2 Put the words in the correct order to make sentences.

1. for/work/is/to/walk/essential/to/me/able/ the/thing/being

   _____

   _____.

2. opportunity/the/having/promotion/vital/is/for

   _____

   _____.

3. major/a/flexible/isn't/having/hours/priority/ working

   _____

   _____.

4. job/is/main/priority/satisfaction/my

   _____

   _____.

5. couldn't/supportive/without/I/co-workers/do/ job/my

   _____

   _____.

6. retirement/really/about/a/not/plan/I'm/ having/concerned

   _____

   _____.

3 Complete the interview with words from the box.

plenty	little	deal	few	vast
handful	most	many	not	

Fun at Work

A: Crocodile curry and cheesy worms may not be everybody's idea of snack food, but MediaCom, rated number 28 in the *Sunday Times* listing of "Top 100 companies to work for," wants to encourage a creative and original take on the world. So, they offer chocolate ants to their workers at break times and have _____ (**1.**) of other interesting ideas, too. With us this morning is Rachel Stanmore, a business expert who has spent some time in this innovative media company. And she's here to tell us more about it. Good morning, Rachel.

B: Good morning.

A: Now I'm _____ (**2.**) much of an expert in these things, so tell me, Rachel, what the company's trying to achieve with these slightly strange ideas?

B: Well, the philosophy is that the company will do better if the workers are inspired. They don't want people coming to work thinking: "Oh, it's just another day at the office."

A: That's a pretty unusual philosophy.

B: Yes, only a _____ (**3.**) of companies do this kind of thing.

A: Can you tell us a _____ (**4.**) bit more about the company?

B: Sure. It's the UK's largest media agency, with 389 employees based in London and Edinburgh. The _____ (**5.**) majority of the workers are young professionals, under 35, who may be earning a great _____ (**6.**) of money, but more importantly, they like to feel appreciated and constantly motivated. For the _____ (**7.**) part they are very supportive of the business, with as _____ (**8.**) as eight out of ten employees feeling excited about where the company's going. And that's because they have control—they know what it's like to run things. Quite a _____ (**9.**) of them have had their own ideas brought into operation. Last year, for example, there was a contest called "If I ran the company," and as a result, a company café was introduced, which provides free breakfasts in the morning, is open until 11:30 at night, and has the boss working behind it.

A: Not bad!

4 Read the interview again and answer the questions on a separate sheet of paper.

1. What is Rachel Stanmore's job?
2. What kind of company is MediaCom?

Grammar

5 Rewrite the sentences using the words in parentheses.

Ex: There is nothing we can do to stop the project. (seemingly)
There is seemingly nothing we can do to stop the project.

1. You may be surprised to hear that sales figures were up from last year. (believe)

   _____

   _____

2. Everyone says that the company is losing a lot of money. (apparently)

   _____

   _____

3. For the most part, the management team has a good relationship with the rest of the employees. (broadly)

   _____

   _____

4. In my opinion, the conclusions of the report are wrong. (fundamentally)

   _____

   _____

5. I'd like to say no to the extra work, but I need the money. (hand)

   _____

   _____

6. What you say is true, but only in part. (point)

   _____

   _____

7. I travel a lot for my job. On the whole, I enjoy it, although it can be exhausting. (large)

   _____

   _____

8. Looking back, we probably should have approached them earlier. (in)

   _____

   _____

9. Unexpectedly, the results of the survey indicate that there could be a good market for the new product. (enough)

   _____

   _____

UNIT 5
Review

1 Match the beginning of the sentence with its end.

____ 1. She hasn't had to worry about money since they sold the business and she came

____ 2. We are paid a fixed salary, plus a 10%

____ 3. He managed to bring the price down by

____ 4 His business went

____ 5. If you know what you are doing, there is plenty of money

____ 6. The house is filled with priceless

____ 7. Ana has worked hard and deserves a

a. bankrupt a few years ago.

b. paintings.

c. commission.

d. raise.

e. to be made on the stock market.

f. into a fortune.

g. haggling with the owner.

2 Complete each sentence by adding a word from the box.

> don't would you as only for

1. If it hadn't been ____ the weather, we would have had a wonderful vacation.

2. You can use my phone, provided that you ____ talk for too long.

3. ____ If I had listened to her advice!

4. Should ____ happen to be in Mexico City, you should call my sister.

5. If you let us know as soon as the package arrives, that ____ be great.

6. As long ____ he lives in that house, I'm not going back there.

3 Choose the correct words to complete each sentence.

1. What ____ when she told us there was no alternative?
   a. she did mean
   b. she means
   c. did she mean

2. I ____ him take the money.
   a. actually saw
   b. saw actually
   c. actual saw

3. They were so relieved to finally buy ____ house.
   a. their own
   b. on their own
   c. own their

4. The journey was ____.
   a. by means no easy
   b. by no means easy
   c. no means by easy

5. ____ impresses me about them is that they are so efficient.
   a. The most thing that
   b. The thing that most
   c. Most the thing that

6. He's not ____.
   a. interested all at soccer
   b. interested in soccer all at
   c. interested in soccer at all

4 Use the clues to complete the crossword.

Across

4. Their ____ was to help the homeless.
6. They spend a ____ on childcare so that they can both go to work.
7. The changes have definitely had a major ____.
11. Take a look at their ____ illustrated catalog.
12. Don't eat any more. You're just being ____.

Down

1. She enjoys ____ money to a good cause.
2. Our ____ is to expand the business over the next five years.
3. Her work has ____ others to join the profession.
5. A wage of $175 a week is hardly enough to ____ for a growing family.
6. The organization was ____ in the mid-1990s.
8. He ____ most of the money into a high-interest bank account.
9. I give all my old clothes to ____.
10. The government has spent a great ____ of money on renovating the old buildings.

5 Complete the sentences using the correct form of the words in parentheses.

1. My work gives me a lot of job _____. (satisfy)
2. Luckily, my boss is very _____. (support)
3. The pay isn't very good initially, but there are good opportunities for _____. (promote)
4. Working under deadlines can be quite _____. (challenge)
5. The company helps with your professional _____. (develop)
6. Having worked at night for so long, it is great to have such _____ working hours. (flex)
7. One of the benefits of the apartment is its _____ location. (convenient)

6 Cross out the choices that are NOT possible, or have a different meaning.

1. We try to support each other, and ____ it seems to work.
   a. by and large   c. broadly speaking
   b. however
2. Transcil always deals with the problem quickly. ____, they do charge a lot for their services.
   a. Essentially   c. However
   b. On the other hand
3. We cut our prices by nearly 50%, and ____ we managed to increase our profits.
   a. believe it or not   c. in hindsight
   b. surprisingly enough
4. She is working for herself and ____ doing very well.
   a. on the other hand   c. seemingly
   b. apparently
5. The business is ____ a technical marketing company.
   a. essentially   c. fundamentally
   b. looking back
6. They moved the factory to China to cut costs. ____, it was the right decision.
   a. In hindsight   c. However
   b. Looking back

UNIT 6
Understanding power

LESSON 1

Reading

1a Read the news story and answer the questions on a separate sheet of paper.

1. What is the purpose of the international vote?
2. What happened to the original seven wonders?

New wonders of the world

They have sheltered kings, protected nations from invaders, inspired the world's greatest artists, and spawned a million postcards. Now the world's most glorified buildings are to be officially recognized, not by the United Nations, or by architects, but by the common man and woman, or at least those with Internet access.

Millions of people are taking part in an international vote to pick seven new wonders of the world. The contenders include: the Statue of Liberty; Petra, in Jordan; the Colosseum; the Acropolis; and the statue of Christ the Redeemer, in Rio de Janeiro. The campaign, via the modern wonder of the Internet, was launched by adventurer, filmmaker, and entrepreneur Bernard Weber, who says he wants to create a definitive list, chosen in a democratic fashion.

After an initial weeding-out process, 21 wonders remain, the final seven of which will be determined by

the number of votes cast in their favor on www.new7wonders.com. The winning sites will be filmed by Mr. Weber. However, not everyone is happy with the short list. The absence of

technology disappointed Stuart Leslie, a professor at Johns Hopkins University. He claims that the Internet should be on the list, simply because it allows us to access all the other wonders. Mr. Leslie's list would also include inventions such as the hydrogen bomb and nylon.

Of the old seven wonders, only one still exists: the Great Pyramid of Giza. The others have been destroyed over the years by a combination of earthquakes, fire, and greed, as invaders ransacked palaces and temples. Though Weber admits he has no idea how long the new seven wonders will last, he's having a lot of fun naming them.

b Read the story again and take notes under the headings.

> The voting process _____
> _____
> Bernard Weber _____
> _____
> Criticisms of the new list _____
> _____

c Circle the best definition. Use the news story to help you.

1. spawn (*v.*)
   a. take photos using advanced technology
   b. inspire others to copy something, or produce or generate something

2. contender (*n.*)
   a. a type of building found in ancient cities
   b. person or thing taking part in a competition

3. definitive (*adj.*)
   a. final/complete/able to serve as a perfect example
   b. long-lasting

4. weed out (*v.*)
   a. remove the worst or weakest from a list or group
   b. put forward an argument for the one you think is the best

5. short list (*n.*)
   a. winner, following a long discussion
   b. group of the best candidates for final consideration (in a competition)

6. ransack (*v.*)
   a. change the structure of a building by adding parts
   b. search violently in order to steal something

Grammar

2 Choose _a_, _an_, _the_, or no article (_–_).

Easter Island

Easter Island is _a/an/the/–_ (**1.**) remote place 2,200 miles off _a/an/the/–_ (**2.**) coast of Chile. It has barely 4,000 inhabitants, one airport, and some simple accommodations for tourists. It used to be full of _a/an/the/–_ (**3.**) lush trees, but they died centuries ago. Yet, Easter Island is world famous. There are few more powerful and mysterious sights than _a/an/the/–_ (**4.**) island's magnificent statues, called moai, rising up out of the barren landscape thirteen feet high and weighing fourteen tons.

These huge stone heads were carved from _a/an/the/–_ (**5.**) volcanic rock between four and nine hundred years ago. With their elongated faces and deep-set eyes, they are _a/an/the/–_ (**6.**) incredibly haunting sight, and there are 887 of them. But what was their purpose?

A/An/The/– (**7.**) archeologists suggest that _a/an/the/–_ (**8.**) statues were symbols of religious and political power, or perhaps depictions of the spirits of early ancestors. There are other mysteries surrounding _a/an/the/–_ (**9.**) moai. They were not built where they are found, so how were they transported? What's more, the majority of the moai have been knocked down and now lie on their faces or in _a/an/the/–_ (**10.**) pieces. Why? We will probably never know.

3 Add or cross out one word to complete each sentence. One sentence is correct.

1. The Taj Mahal is probably most famous building in India.
2. The Ice Hotel, in Quebec, is made up entirely from ice.
3. Maya Ying Lin designed a famous wall in Washington, D.C. as memorial for the soldiers who died in Vietnam.
4. The Arc de Triomphe, in Paris, was built honor of Napoleon's military conquests.
5. Covering an area of a million square feet, Paris's Pompidou Center is one of Europe's greatest cultural centers.
6. The Great Wall of China is about 4,000 miles long and eight yards up high.
7. The Mayan pyramids may have been used for to house the bodies of kings.
8. Turkey's greatest church, the Hagia Sophia, is said to have built in just five years.

Writing

4 Read the notes about two pieces of architecture that didn't go according to plan. Choose one and write a short essay about it. Use phrases from page 70 of the Student Book to help you.

Leaning Tower of Pisa
— a bell tower, next to Pisa Cathedral, Pisa, Italy
— started 1173, completed 1372 (wars prevented completion)
— architect: Pisano and di Simone + others??
— problem: tower began to sink during construction, as soil settled
— 1272: engineers built upper floors with one side taller than the other to compensate for building's tilt
— 1990–2001: closed for repairs and reconstruction. Now stable for next 300 years.

Empire State Building
— skyscraper, New York City, USA
— started 1930, opened May 1, 1931
— architect: William F. Lamb
— problem: strong winds made building unstable
— builders designed special framework
— building became so solid that it was easily repaired when a plane crashed into it in 1945!

Reading

1a Read the article quickly and choose the best sub-heading.

1. How technology is changing the way our students learn
2. Email etiquette in college
3. How professors and students keep in touch

Student power

(1) One student skipped class and then sent the professor an email message asking for copies of the teaching notes. Another didn't like her grade and sent a petulant message to the professor. Another explained that she was late for a Monday class because she was recovering from a party. One professor received a message from a student, saying "I'm not sure how to shop for school supplies. Should I buy a binder or a subject notebook? Would you let me know your recommendations?" At colleges and universities, email has made professors more approachable, but many say it has made them too accessible. They say that students seem to view them as available around the clock, sending a steady stream of email messages—from ten a week to ten after every class—that are too informal or simply inappropriate. Michael J. Kessler, a lecturer at Georgetown University, says, "The tone that they take in an email is pretty astounding, 'I need to know this and you need to tell me right now.' It's a fine balance to accommodate what they need and at the same time maintain a level of legitimacy as an instructor. We are authorized to make demands on them, and not the other way around."

(2) Professor Patricia Ewick, of Clark University, Massachusetts, said ten students emailed her drafts of their papers days before they were due, seeking comments. Ewick says, "It's all different levels of presumption. One is that I'll be able to drop everything and read 250 pages two days before I'm going to get fifty of these." Robert B. Ahdieh, associate professor of law, said he had received emails with messages such as "you're covering the material too fast" or "I don't think we're using the reading as much as we could in class" or "I think it would be helpful if you would summarize what we've covered at the end of class in case we missed anything." While once professors expected deference, their expertise seems to have become just another service that students, as consumers, are buying. So, students may have no fear of giving offense or imposing on the professor's time. Many professors say they are uncertain

how to react to the emails. For example, the professor who was asked about buying the notebook said she debated whether to tell the student that this was not a query that should be directed to her, but worried that "such a message could be pretty scary" and decided not to respond at all.

(3) Most professors, however, emphasized that instant feedback could be invaluable. One professor said that questions about a lecture or discussion indicated "a blind spot," that the student obviously didn't understand something. Others have probably hit on the best solution by making rules for email: telling students how quickly the professor would respond, how messages should be drafted, and what type of messages they would answer. Meg Worley, an assistant professor of English, tells students that they must say thank you after receiving a professor's response to an email. "The less powerful person always has to write back," she said.

b Complete the notes using information from the article.

- In higher education, professors are now more _____ (1.) than they used to be because of _____ (2.).
- The problem: students either write too _____ (3.) emails or write emails that are _____ (4.) (maybe too informal or thoughtless).
- Kessler says he doesn't like the _____ (5.) of the emails he receives.
- Ewick thinks that students these days _____ (6.) too much and seem to think that their teachers have a lot of free _____ (7.).
- Ahdieh received criticisms of his _____ (8.) by email.
- A lot of professors aren't _____ (9.) how to respond to these emails.
- Some professors have solved the problem by making _____ (10.) about email use.

c Check the sentences that are true, according to the article.

_____ 1. The professors said that students rarely <u>missed</u> lessons without good reasons. (paragraph 1)

_____ 2. Some students write <u>angry</u> emails and behave like children. (paragraph 1)

_____ 3. As a professor, you have to maintain your <u>credibility</u> in front of students. (paragraph 1)

_____ 4. One professor asked students to email the first <u>version</u> of their compositions. (paragraph 2)

_____ 5. Students' emails show that the traditional <u>humility toward</u> professors isn't as common as it used to be. (paragraph 2)

_____ 6. Many professors said that receiving criticisms by email was <u>extremely useful</u> to them. (paragraph 3)

_____ 7. Emails about lectures sometimes showed there was <u>an area that the student didn't grasp very well</u>. (paragraph 3)

_____ 8. Some professors <u>found a perfect answer to the problem</u> by banning email correspondence. (paragraph 3)

d Find words or expressions in the article that have the same meaning as the underlined words or expressions in Exercise 1c.

Grammar

2 Six of these sentences contain mistakes. Check the correct sentences and correct the mistakes in the others.

_____ 1. I'll vote for who has the best economic plan.

_____ 2. Roberto is your driver. Where you want to go, he will take you.

_____ 3. Whatever we want to do, we have to get permission from the boss.

_____ 4. How you look at it, whether you are an employee or a customer, it's a stupid rule.

_____ 5. Whenever the teacher comes into the room, the students stand up.

_____ 6. What you said, I didn't hear you because of the music.

_____ 7. I'll talk to whoever I can in order to get you an interview.

_____ 8. Who you spoke to, it wasn't the boss, but an impersonator!

_____ 9. Help me however you can.

_____ 10. Wherever I go, that beautiful woman seems to follow.

_____ 11. How you choose to join, whether online or in person, it is a great deal.

3 Circle the correct choices to complete the paragraph.

Parent Power

Desperate parents in Gigo, New Zealand, decided to write a manifesto for the children in the town, following a rise in bad behavior. "I'm not sure _why/however_ (**1.**) it got so bad, but _whatever/whenever_ (**2.**) one of us tried to discipline our kids, they would just swear at us," says Joe Malonga. "_Whatever/However_ (**3.**) we tried to do, it failed. We tried bribing them, punishing them, and eventually begging them. Nothing worked." So, _whenever/when_ (**4.**) Malonga suggested drawing up a list of rules, other parents agreed immediately. "_Who/Whoever_ (**5.**) thought of a rule had to be backed by 70% of the parents. Then, we persuaded the kids to sign the document, and posted hundreds of copies around town." _Where/Wherever_ (**6.**) you look—in stores, schools, bus stops—you can see Gigo's Twelve Golden Rules. "So far it's worked like a charm," says Malonga.

Vocabulary

4 Circle the correct word or words to complete each sentence.

1. This is our new product. We're hoping it will catch in Asia especially.

   a. up   b. off   c. on

2. Revolutions tend to come because of desperation on a huge scale.

   a. through   b. on   c. about

3. According to fashion guru Leila Winston, lacy stockings are this winter, and every woman should have a pair.

   a. off   b. in   c. up

4. It can be difficult to keep the news on the island, because the mail only comes once a month, and there's no Internet.

   a. up with   b. up to   c. on with

5. The company decided to home new technology, focusing its attention on digital software.

   a. in to   b. in on   c. up to

6. While hats were trendy last summer, they seem to be this year.

   a. on   b. off   c. out

Communication

1 Read the conversation on the right. Then mark the statements true (*T*) or false (*F*).

_____ 1. Pete thinks that people sometimes confuse fame and charisma.

_____ 2. Joan doesn't like movie stars much.

_____ 3. Joan thinks athletes are often charismatic.

_____ 4. Joan believes that most politicians have a little bit of charisma.

_____ 5. Ann is surprised by Joan's opinions.

Grammar

2 Cross out the choice that is NOT possible.

1. The waiter didn't bring the food until midnight, *by which time/at which point/despite* Sarah was starving.

2. *No sooner had I arrived than/I'd hardly arrived when/On arriving*, Don left.

3. *Although/When/While* we like pasta, we don't want to eat it every day.

4. He finished the race *despite/even though/although* he felt sick.

5. We can't understand your theory, *much as/in spite/hard as* we try.

6. *On falling asleep/She hardly falls asleep/No sooner does she fall asleep than* she starts snoring.

7. No one goes to bed before 2 A.M. *during the festival/while the festival is going on/as long as the festival is*.

8. *Although/Despite/In spite of* your behavior, everyone had a good time yesterday.

Charisma . . . same as fame?

Pete: I'm never quite sure if people are really charismatic or if it's just something having to do with fame. Being famous kind of makes you automatically charismatic.

Ann: Like when a movie star walks into a restaurant, you mean, and everyone turns and stares and says: "Oh, what charisma," but actually it's just that the person's famous.

Pete: Exactly.

Joan: I think most famous people actually have no charisma whatsoever. Most movie stars are short, ugly, boring, and self-obsessed, which is just another way of being boring, of course.

Pete: Do you really think so?

Joan: Oh yeah, half of them are tiny. And they have bad skin.

Ann: Well, athletes are usually pretty impressive, physically.

Joan: True, but they don't have anything to say. They spend their whole lives in the gym, so as soon as they open their mouths, out comes a stream of nonsense.

Pete: But don't you think some of them are charismatic? Muhammad Ali or Pelé, people like that.

Joan: No.

Ann: What do you mean "no"?!

Joan: Well, if it wasn't for his achievements in a boxing ring, Ali would just be a loudmouth. I don't think that's charismatic at all. Same with all performing artists. They are good at one thing and then everyone assumes that they have some magical, mystical power like charisma. I don't buy it.

Pete: OK.

Ann: OK, well what about politicians? They must have some charisma in order for people to follow them.

Joan: Are you kidding? I'd say about .01% of politicians are charismatic. Most of them have lots of money behind them and a big political party that tells them what to say and wear and do, and how many babies to kiss.

Ann: I never knew you were so cynical, Joan.

3 Circle the best words or phrases below to complete the paragraphs.

Smart cop

An instructor had been explaining leadership to a group of police recruits from 8:00 to 1:00, ____ (**1.**) they were tired and hungry. Finally, the instructor gave one man secret instructions that he had to "get everyone out of here without causing panic." The recruit didn't know what to do. The instructor called a second man to the front. ____ (**2.**) the note, the recruit said, "The instructor wants us to go outside. Go!" No one moved. A third man looked at the instructions, smiled and said, "Break for lunch!" ____ (**3.**) the room emptied in seconds.

Mozart's Memory

When Mozart was a boy, his father took him to Rome. ____ (**4.**) their trip, they attended a service at St. Peter's Cathedral. Part of the music used in the service was a highly guarded secret, never shared with outsiders. As they listened, Mozart's father noticed his son's fascination with the music. That night, they ____ (**5.**) home when Mozart sat down and played the entire musical score, note for note. ____ (**6.**) the Vatican's best efforts, the secret was no match for Mozart's incredible memory!

A new page

Incredibly ____ (**9.**), Google is no traditional workplace, and co-founder Larry Page is said to be a charismatic, as well as unorthodox, boss. Page once made the staff attend a meeting wearing pink wigs, and he even tried to ban phones from a Google building. ____ (**10.**), he was told that the law required a phone in the elevators.

Thirsty soldiers

____ (**7.**) marching across the desert with his thirsty army, Alexander the Great was offered a helmet of water by one of his soldiers. Alexander said, "Is there enough for 10,000 men?" The soldier had no answer, and ____ (**8.**) Alexander was dying of thirst himself, he poured the water onto the ground.

1. **a.** by this time **b.** at this time **c.** by which time
2. **a.** By reading **b.** On reading **c.** To read
3. **a.** at which point **b.** at this point **c.** to the point that
4. **a.** While **b.** In the middle **c.** During
5. **a.** had hardly returned **b.** was already return **c.** had sooner returned

6. **a.** Although **b.** In spite **c.** Despite
7. **a.** During **b.** While **c.** On
8. **a.** in spite of **b.** much as **c.** even though
9. **a.** successful as is **b.** successful as it is **c.** as it is successful
10. **a.** However **b.** He'd hardly started **c.** Even though

Vocabulary

4 Complete the puzzle and find the key word. Look on page 76 of the Student Book if necessary.

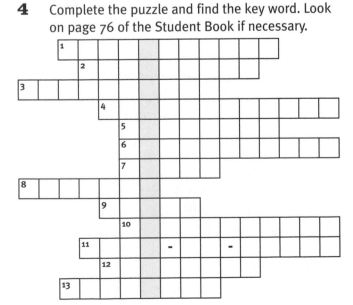

1. has a magnetic character that makes people want to follow (*adj.*)
2. is well-respected because he or she is calm and serious (*adj.*)
3. believes people should live according to high moral standards and principles (*adj.*)
4. is easy to talk to and friendly (*adj.*)
5. never stops working because he or she has lots of energy (*adj.*)
6. can be trusted completely (*adj.*)
7. is unable to make a decision, often ____s (*v.*)
8. accepts money illegally for favors (*adj.*)
9. is energetic and determined, has ____ (*n.*)
10. is not recognizable or interesting (*adj.*)
11. is practical and direct in a sensible, honest way (*adj.*)
12. is respected for his or her intellectual seriousness, has ____ (*n.*)
13. is determined and won't change his or her mind (*adj.*)

Key word _____

1 Each of these sentences has one or two mistakes. Find the mistakes and correct them.

1. The dogs are generally considered the best pets for the elderly.

2. We thought we heard burglar, but later we realized that a noise was actually the pipes.

3. He climbed the Mt. Kilimanjaro when he was still the teenager.

4. As a child, she learned to play a piano and later went on to become the composer.

5. I'll see you at a supermarket at 8:00. Don't be late!

6. It's hard for the people like me to diet, because we love the chocolate.

7. Canada has introduced law to help newly-arrived immigrants find work.

8. I dreamed that I crossed Pacific Ocean in an old wooden boat!

9. Italian national anthem is one of my favorites.

10. We spoke to CEO of the company last night.

2 Circle the correct sentence(s) in each pair. Both may be correct.

1. a. Who you are, come out now with your hands up!
   b. Whoever you are, come out now with your hands up!

2. a. However hard I tried, it was never good enough for my father.
   b. How hard I tried, it was never good enough for my father.

3. a. You'll need to explain whatever you did, in very clear English.
   b. You'll need to explain what you did, in very clear English.

4. a. When you want to come over, just give me a call.
   b. Whenever you want to come over, just give me a call.

5. a. It seems that whichever option we choose, it's going to be costly.
   b. It seems that which option we choose, it's going to be costly.

6. a. This pocket knife will be useful where you're going.
   b. This pocket knife will be useful wherever you're going.

3 Circle the correct word or expression.

A friend forever

Desperate, Nick Bines broke into the home of a wealthy businessman, intending to steal jewelry and other valuables. He had _hardly/sooner_ (**1.**) begun the burglary when he looked at the sideboard and, to his surprise, saw himself in a framed photo. The photo showed a group of teenagers on a fishing trip. Bines went to the living room and looked at other photos on display, _although/at which point_ (**2.**) he realized that he was robbing the home of his best friend from school, Michael Pasha, whom he hadn't seen for ten years. _Much/Hard_ (**3.**) as he needed the money, Bines decided to put everything back in its place. He had begun to climb out of the window _whenever/when_ (**4.**) he caught his leg on the frame, fell, and broke his ankle. He _had no sooner/by this time_ (**5.**) started crawling away along the side of the street than Michael Pasha's car pulled up. _Although/On_ (**6.**) seeing his old friend in this state, Pasha took Bines inside. _In spite of the fact/While_ (**7.**) they were talking, it soon became obvious what had happened. _In spite/Despite_ (**8.**) of this, instead of reporting his old friend to the police, Pasha took Bines to the hospital, and a month later, gave him a job.

4 Match the beginning of each sentence to its end.

_____ 1. I'd walked for six hours, at

_____ 2. Much as I love him,

_____ 3. I passed the exam in spite

_____ 4. I'd no sooner

_____ 5. Although my alarm didn't go off,

_____ 6. I'd hardly started my journey

_____ 7. It took me until 2:00 to find her number, by which

_____ 8. Hard as I

a. when my tire exploded.

b. tried, I just couldn't finish the race.

c. taken off my coat than it started raining.

d. time she'd arrived.

e. of the fact that I felt awful.

f. I still woke up early.

g. which point I was absolutely starving.

h. I really don't want to get married now.

5 Rewrite the sentences using the correct form of the word in parentheses.

1. You must stay up-to-date with developments in your field. (keep)

   You must _____

   _____.

2. Those pants are trendy these days. (in)

   Those pants _____.

3. The idea originated because of something I read. (come)

   The idea _____

   _____.

4. The company is targeting the children's market. (home)

   The company is _____

   _____.

5. That fashion will grow popular very quickly. (catch)

   That fashion will _____

   _____.

6. Style gurus tell us that long hair is no longer in style. (out)

   Style gurus tell us that long hair _____.

6 Complete the news headlines with words from the box.

> consumer   brain   in positions   wind
> comes to   world   special powers

1. Scientists hail _____ power as answer to energy crisis.

2. Ten-year-old genius uses _____ power to solve ancient puzzle!

3. China is fast emerging as the new _____ power.

4. Supermarket boss says _____ power is forcing food companies to "go organic" as customers walk away.

5. Report says corruption is on the rise among people _____ of power.

6. Political party _____ power after twenty years in the wilderness.

7. Government grants _____ to anti-terrorist squad.

7 Circle the best words or phrases below to complete the paragraph.

Chad Thomson is _____ (1.) speaker—he had the audience in the palm of his hand at the Clovell Center on Tuesday. His theme was that business leaders no longer have to be incredibly _____ (2.); the era of the superhero CEO is over. Leaders today need to be _____ (3.) and _____ (4.) in order to understand the challenges faced by workers. Bosses that remain _____ (5.), locking themselves away in the office, are less effective. Thomson also said that _____ (6.) leaders who regularly work 18-hour days are disappearing. His other theme was decision-making. Leaders who _____ (7.) in the face of problems are not real leaders, while those who remain _____ (8.) while under pressure are.

1. a. a gravitas   c. an aloof
   b. an inspiring

2. a. nondescript   c. charismatic
   b. dignity

3. a. corrupt   c. approachable
   b. approached

4. a. down-to-earth   c. lacking in energy
   b. charisma

5. a. inspirational   c. aloof
   b. idealistic

6. a. trustworthy   c. tiring
   b. tireless

7. a. wave   c. waver
   b. drive

8. a. powerful   c. trusted
   b. resolute

The natural world

Reading

1a Read the article below. Then answer the questions.

1. What do Jiggs, Bart, Rock of Gibraltar and Keela have in common?

   _____
   _____

2. Why might the chief of the South Yorkshire Police Force be jealous of Keela?

   _____
   _____

3. What do the police use Keela for?

   _____
   _____

4. What were the FBI interested in?

   _____
   _____

b Find words in the article that mean:

1. paid for a job or service (*v.*) (paragraph 1)

   _____

2. very small amounts of something (*n.*) (paragraph 2) _____

3. cleaned (by rubbing it) (*v.*) (paragraph 2)

   _____

4. extremely small (*adj.*) (paragraph 2)

   _____

5. to improve a skill so that it is done very well (*v.*) (paragraph 3) _____

6. no angry thoughts (three words, idiomatic) (paragraph 4) _____

c Cover the article. Match a word from A to a word from B to make phrases from the text.

A	chief	training	crime	sense
	movie	laundry	dog	in

B	star	of police	of smell	detergent
	scene	handlers	regimen	demand

d Complete the summary of the article. Use the phrases you made in Exercise 1c.

She may not be a _____ (1.) like other high-earning animals, but Keela is similarly _____ (2.). She has an incredible _____ (3.); she can detect blood even after clothes have been washed in _____ (4.). This makes her especially useful at a _____ (5.). Once the _____ (6.) realized she was so exceptional, they invented a special _____ (7.) for her. She now makes more money than the _____ (8.)!

The dog with the golden nose

(1) Jiggs, the chimpanzee who starred in over fifteen Tarzan movies in the 1930s, was paid thousands of dollars. The owner of Bart, an Alaskan brown bear, was paid a million dollars for letting Bart appear in the film *The Edge.* A racehorse called Rock of Gibraltar is worth an estimated $170 million. And now there is Keela, a dog doing a great job and getting well remunerated for it.

(2) The spaniel is no movie star, but she has become so important for South Yorkshire Police in England, that she now earns more than the chief of police. The secret of her success? Keela has an astonishing sense of smell. She can sniff traces of blood on weapons that have been scrubbed clean after attacks and even on clothes that have been washed repeatedly in biological laundry detergent. PC Ellis, Keela's handler, said, "She can detect minute quantities of blood that cannot be seen with the human eye. She is used at crime scenes where someone has tried to clean it up."

(3) Once they realized Keela had these extraordinary skills, the dog handlers used a special training regimen to hone her talent. In fact, her training was so successful that the FBI has inquired about it.

(4) Not surprisingly, Keela is in demand with other crime-busters. For her services, other police forces are charged $850 a day, plus expenses. She earns the South Yorkshire Police Force around $320,000 a year, more than PC Hughes, her boss! Hughes says there are no hard feelings. "Keela's training gives the police force an edge when it comes to forensic investigation which we should recognize and use more often."

Grammar

2 Circle the correct word or phrase to complete each sentence.

1. Jan wants to eat at Bob's Kitchen or King Curry House, ____ appeals to me.
   a. neither which   c. neither of which
   b. of neither which

2. I met the writer Kate Atkinson, ____ books made such an impression on me.
   a. of which   b. whose   c. with whose

3. The lead actor, ____ the show depended, didn't turn up.
   a. who on   b. on whom   c. who

4. Carrie left early, ____ seems strange to me since she usually loves parties.
   a. that   b. which   c. who

5. Zadie, ____ five children are brilliant mathematicians, is no good at math.
   a. of whose   b. who's   c. whose

6. The party leader, ____ asked to justify himself, could not.
   a. when   b. who   c. while

3 Complete the sentences using ideas from the box, plus *who*, *when*, *which*, or *whom*. You may need to add a preposition.

Ex: There were a hundred guests, most _of whom_
        I'd already met.

> know/the way   I/buy/yesterday
> eat/all/chocolate   be/interested
> work OK/now   meet/ already
> brother/work/with my wife

1. It was Juan _____.
   That's why he's feeling sick!

2. When I was lost, I asked four people, none
   _____.

3. These books, _____,
   got really great reviews.

4. Last week, we fixed these computers, all
   _____.

5. This form must be completed before the conference. Please check the topic in
   _____.

6. I spoke to the woman _____
   _____.

Vocabulary

4 One word in each sentence belongs in another sentence. Find the words and cross them out. Then write them in the correct sentences.

1. By watching the movements of animals, we can predict natural safety, such as earthquakes and tidal waves.

2. There are many stories of drowning people being carried to instincts by dolphins; these may be true because dolphins rescue animals the same size as themselves.

3. Animal disasters often allow animals to escape from danger that humans don't notice.

4. Rescue teams work with dogs because of the dogs' excellent invisible of smell.

5. Birds used to save sense during wartime by carrying vital messages to army commanders.

6. In the dark, cats and bats see things that are lives to the human eye.

5 Complete the article by adding words from the box.

> tricky   once   this   step   if
> straightforward   put   need   of

Teaching a parrot to talk

Bird expert Olaf Sund says that teaching a parrot to talk is a piece cake. Here, he gives a few invaluable tips.

The first thing you to do is choose the right bird. Bigger birds, like Blue Fronts and Yellow Napes, are your best bet, and make sure you get them when they are young. Birds older than 18 months probably won't learn to talk.

You've chosen the bird, put it in the room where the family congregates the most—maybe the living room. For parrots to learn how to talk, human interaction is the key.

At first, it can be a little for any wild animal in a domestic environment, so give the bird a few weeks to acclimate. The next is to turn off the TV and remove any distractions. Place the bird on your hand and say a word in conjunction with an action or object. For example, give it a peanut and say: "Peanut" or lift the bird up and say: "Up." The process must be pretty, so use short, simple words at first.

Be gentle and patient with the bird, and lots of emotion in your voice. Teach the bird in 15-minute sessions, and give rewards, such as food, when the bird repeats a word. Without doing, some birds are slow to speak. Your teaching doesn't work, you should allow another family member to try. Many birds prefer a female voice.

Reading

1a Read the three excerpts from *Extreme Landscapes* on the right. Write questions for the answers.

1. _____?

   Because they know where the water is.

2. _____?

   Because, by looking at them, you will see how the landscape has changed over millions of years.

3. _____?

   Like a person or animal roaring.

4. _____?

   Behind the water, next to the rock face.

5. _____?

   Captain Cook's.

6. _____?

   60,000 years old.

7. _____?

   Because a coral reef is actually alive.

b Answer the questions on a separate sheet of paper.

Death Valley

1. Why does the writer mention a man frying an egg on a car?

2. Why do you think he says "You grow a new skin?"

The Iguaçu Falls

3. What images connected with the voice does the writer use to describe the Iguaçu Falls?

4. Why does he "wonder if [the birds] can ever hear themselves sing?"

The Great Barrier Reef

5. The writer calls the Great Barrier Reef "a million jewels." What do you think he means?

c Find words in the excerpts that mean:

1. burning brightly (excerpt 1) _____

2. crawl desperately, with your face to the ground (excerpt 1) _____

3. an enormous hole in the surface of the earth (excerpt 2) _____

4. forced into a small space (excerpt 2) _____

5. waterfall (excerpt 2) _____

6. crashed (excerpt 3) _____

7. long pieces of heavy wood used in buildings and ships (excerpt 3) _____

8. clear, transparent, allowing light to pass through (excerpt 3) _____

The Great Barrier Reef

The Iguaçu Falls

Death Valley

1: Death Valley

Don't get me wrong. I've seen a man fry an egg on the hood of his car in Arizona. I've seen birds drop dead out of the sky from the heat. I've seen acres of cracked Sudanese earth and the jawbone of a wildebeest fifty miles from the nearest water. But nothing can prepare you for Death Valley in the depths of a blazing summer. Everywhere you look, the air is shaking like fire. You grovel for water, following the trails of wise animals, keeping your distance. You grow a new skin, like leather.

The joy of Death Valley is in the rocks. Look closely and you'll see the history of the world. Burned into those rocks are the stories of climate change, the mutations of wind, water, and gravity since the beginning of time.

2: The Iguaçu Falls

What hits you first is the sound. Long before you get close, you hear the roaring, like some great giant's endless breath. As you approach, it gets louder, until finally you see it—a vast chasm beyond your imagining, endless tongues of screaming white water and spray rebounding a hundred feet into the air. The Iguaçu Falls. I look over the edge and I see behind the water, jammed against the rock, birds' nests! A whole colony of them. They made their home in the middle of the world's biggest cataract. And now, twisting like corkscrews from under the spray, the birds rise free into the air and float above us. I wonder if they can ever hear themselves sing.

3: The Great Barrier Reef

In 1770, Captain Cook's boat rammed smack into the reef. A barrel of rum fell overboard and sank. Little did he know that underneath the wooden beams of his ship there was a world of such magnificence, such translucent light and life. The Great Barrier Reef is a million jewels. Flatback turtles and humpback whales, dolphins and clownfish and giant clams with sprawling shells. The Great Barrier Reef is a poem to itself: 1,243 miles (2,000 kilometers) long and 60,000 years old, 900 islands and 3,000 coral reefs. They say you can see it from space.

I duck beneath the water for the twentieth time, the scuba tank heavy on my back. I am still trying to believe my eyes. The water is like a glass kaleidoscope, a riot of color. This is the biggest living organism in the world, and I am swimming in its blue heart.

Grammar

2 Match each sentence or phrase to the statement that could follow it.

1. _____ 1. She remembers talking to Joe.
   _____ 2. She remembered to talk to Joe.
   a. At the last party she accidentally ignored him.
   b. They were outside the library.

2. _____ 1. I regret telling you about the accident.
   _____ 2. I regret to tell you about the accident.
   a. I should have kept it a secret.
   b. Fortunately, nobody has been seriously hurt.

3. _____ 1. Huan tried drinking the special remedy,
   _____ 2. Huan tried to drink the special remedy,
   a. but he couldn't swallow it because it was so disgusting.
   b. but it didn't cure him of his illness.

4. _____ 1. The old man stopped listening to the birds.
   _____ 2. The old man stopped to listen to the birds.
   a. They were singing beautifully so he stayed there for a while.
   b. They were making such a terrible noise that he couldn't stand it any more.

5. _____ 1. Since the children liked his first game,
   _____ 2. After buying his first Lego set at the age of eight,
   a. he continued inventing games all afternoon until everyone had had enough.
   b. he went on to invent lots of games, and eventually he became famous.

3 Complete the story below using the correct form of words from the box.

> | experience | travel | make | go |
> | become | leave | take | stay |

Life choices

She remembered _____ (**1.**) that photo. It was the first day of her trip in the desert. While her friends were content to sit on a beach during their vacations, she always tried _____ (**2.**) new customs, new places, new people. She used to say, "The day I stop _____ (**3.**) the world is the day I die." Her parents thought she would go on _____ (**4.**) either a travel writer or a tour guide, but instead, one day, she just never returned.

On a trip to Egypt, she had stopped _____ (**5.**) for a camel ride near the Pyramids in Cairo. She had never meant _____ (**6.**) longer than a day or two, but as she watched the sun slowly falling over the sand dunes, casting them in a sea of orange, she fell in love with the desert and vowed to stay. It meant _____ (**7.**) behind the safe world that she had known all her life, but now, 40 years later, sitting at her home in Alexandria, looking over the photos, it was a choice she has never regretted _____ (**8.**).

Vocabulary

4 Match the beginning of each sentence with its end.

_____ 1. Fish River Canyon probably has the most spectacular

_____ 2. I thought Siberia would have been too cold for permanent

_____ 3. Disneyland is one of the world's most visited tourist

_____ 4. There are a number of active

_____ 5. Death Valley in California is 282 feet below

_____ 6. Many places in Arkansas became ghost

_____ 7. I like Rio's vibrant

a. volcanoes in Italy, including Mount Vesuvius.

b. towns after a terrible epidemic killed 70,000 people.

c. landscape in Africa. It's the world's second biggest canyon.

d. nightlife. There's always a party going on somewhere.

e. settlement, but there are large communities that live there.

f. sites—millions see it every year.

g. sea level.

Grammar

1 Match the questions to the answers.

_____ 1. How many pictures should we take?

_____ 2. Who's going to be there?

_____ 3. What do the expensive tickets cost?

_____ 4. How far is it to Jacksonville?

_____ 5. Do you go there regularly?

_____ 6. What have you heard about me?

_____ 7. How tall is he?

_____ 8. Can I have some of your water?

a. Yes, as much as you like.

b. Over $100.

c. Virtually everyone.

d. Virtually nothing.

e. Well, less than ten miles.

f. Approximately six feet.

g. As many as we can.

h. As often as possible.

2 Circle the word or phrase that could be or should be added to the sentence.

1. I'm told that all of them passed—only two people had to retake the exam.
   a. majority   **c.** virtually
   b. precisely

2. Our classes cost $224.99 per week, an absolute bargain!
   a. as much as   **c.** as little as
   b. as many as

3. Your suitcase weighs 50 pounds, which is the limit!
   a. well over   **c.** a minimum
   b. much above

4. This elevator takes ten people.
   a. a majority of   **c.** virtually
   b. a maximum of

5. A people wanted Jones to win, but everyone else voted for Smith.
   a. small majority   **c.** few of
   b. tiny minority of

6. During the winter, we sometimes get two or three tourist groups a week.
   a. as little as   **c.** as few as
   b. a great deal of

7. I need 123 of those bottles. No more, no less!
   a. precisely   **c.** a minimum of
   b. approximately

Vocabulary

3 Each monolog has two mistakes. Find the mistakes and correct them.

1. "Well, yes, it's used, but it's in great condition. This really is a rare opportunity because it's a latest model, as I'm sure you realize. Everything's in working order, although I haven't tried the brakes yet. And don't worry about that tear and wear on the tires. They'll be fine."

2. "This one is a very rare opal stone. It really is one in a kind. Over a thousand years ago, it was probably worn by a tribal queen. Despite its age, you can see that it is in perfect conditions."

3. "This model has only been on the markets for a few weeks and it's unbelievable; you've got wide-screen vision, anti-reflection technology, and it even features an intelligent remote control that knows your viewing tastes. It's absolutely state-in-the-art and it's yours, brand new, for just $10,000."

4. "OK, OK, they're second-hand but they're as well as new. I mean, look, they're still in the original packaging! They come in a wide arrangement of colors and sizes, and the lenses are just fantastic. What do you mean, 'the sun's not going to come out'?"

5. "These are all made to hand. We pick the fruit in the morning, chop it up and coat it in sugar and honey. Then, we roll the pastry and put the fruit inside it. You can choose from a selecting of over fifteen fruits."

Writing

4 Choose one of the pictures below. Imagine you are selling the item(s) online. Write the ad on a separate sheet of paper.

Communication

5a Read the statements. Check the response that best describes your view.

1. Scientists should be banned from doing medical experiments on animals.

   1 = agree completely   2 = it depends   3 = disagree completely
   ⟵◻——————◻——————◻⟶

2. People who mistreat their pets should go to prison.

   1 = agree completely   2 = it depends   3 = disagree completely
   ⟵◻——————◻——————◻⟶

3. Animals should not be put in circuses or used for other forms of entertainment.

   1 = agree completely   2 = it depends   3 = disagree completely
   ⟵◻——————◻——————◻⟶

b Read the interviews on the right. For each interview, answer the following questions. Use a separate sheet of paper.

1. What is his or her job?
2. Has the speaker (or his or her profession) been criticized? If so, what for?
3. Does the speaker justify this treatment of animals? If so, how?
4. How does the interviewer feel about the issue? How do we know?

Ethical dilemmas

Interview 1

A: Jennifer, you say your profession is under attack, but isn't it the mice, the monkeys, and the other animals, that are suffering?

B: I realize the ethics of it aren't simple, but to have people burning down labs and threatening the families of scientists is something else entirely.

A: Three million experiments on animals were conducted in the US alone last year, in the name of science. How can we possibly justify those sorts of numbers?

B: Well, first, I would dispute those figures. But the main point is that the experiments are for the benefit of humankind. Without them, we'd be much worse off. No one wants to harm an animal intentionally, but you have to weigh a number of issues.

Interview 2

A: Heather, you've written, and I'm quoting here, that you "see the darker side of humanity every day." Can you explain what you mean by that?

C: Well, I work for the Humane Society, a charity that protects animals. I go wherever there are abuses of animals, and some of the things I see are very shocking.

A: Could you give us an example?

C: I could give you thousands. A week ago, I discovered that a family had locked up a large dog in a four-by-four-foot cupboard for one week, without giving it food or water. So, that's what I mean by the darker side of humanity.

A: It seems impossible in this day and age that these things can still happen, doesn't it?

Interview 3

D: It had always been one of the great traditions of our circus, but eventually the pressure became too great.

A: And that's why you stopped using animals?

D: For myself, and a number of other circus managers, it was obvious that times had changed. But it wasn't an easy decision to get rid of animals from our act.

A: What effects has the decision had?

D: Well, the first thing was that I had to fire about 50 members of the staff whose job was taking care of or training the animals, and that was very tough for them and me. The second thing was that little children would come to the circus expecting to see monkeys and elephants and sea lions, and they wouldn't be there.

A: Do you believe it was wrong to use the animals in the circus, when we know they were taken from their natural environment and basically captured and trained to entertain people?

D: No. The animals were treated extremely well. It was pressure from outside that forced the decision on me.

1 Find words in Unit 7 of the Student Book that match the definitions. The first letter is given.

1. a_____ = many medical scientists do ____ *testing* before testing medicines on humans (*n.*)

2. b_____ = animals do this to have offspring (*v.*) OR particular type in a species of animal (*n.*)

3. c_____ = meat eater (*n.*)

4. d_____ = animal that can smell a bomb (*n.*)

5. e_____ = ____ *species* are types of animal which may become extinct soon (*adj.*)

6. f_____ = *the* ____ *trade* uses precious animal skin for clothing (*n.*)

7. h_____ = an animal's ____ is the place where wild animals live (*n.*)

8. h_____ = when humans pursue and kill an animal for food (*v.*)

9. i_____ = animal ____ allow animals to sense danger (*n.*)

10. l_____ = an expanse of land seen from one view point (*n.*)

11. m_____ = animal that feeds its young with milk from its body (e.g. cows, humans) (*n.*)

12. o_____ = when humans catch too many fish in one place, leading to changes in the ecosystem (*v.*)

13. p_____ = any animal that hunts another (*n.*)

14. r_____ = a *nature* ____ is an area of land where wild animals are protected (*n.*)

15. s_____ = area for birds or animals where they are safe and can't be hunted (*n.*)

16. v_____ = you and your pet may need one to avoid diseases (*n.*)

17. w_____ = spider's home OR where you can buy animals illegally (*n.*)

2 Circle the phrase to finish each sentence. Both choices may be correct.

1. I went to greet the children, some ____.
   a. of whom I'd already met
   b. of them I'd already met

2. We visited the two proposed sites, ____.
   a. of which neither was appropriate
   b. neither of which was appropriate

3. I went bowling last night, ____.
   a. that was enjoyable
   b. which was enjoyable

4. That's the multinational corporation ____.
   a. for which she worked
   b. which she worked for

5. That's the singer ____.
   a. whose CD you're always playing
   b. who's CD you're always playing

6. There must be a hundred lights in here, ____.
   a. none of them work
   b. none of which work

7. We are walking the same path ____.
   a. that Robert Frost walked
   b. which Robert Frost walked

8. This is one law ____.
   a. which we all benefit from
   b. from which we all benefit

9. It's a profession ____.
   a. in that I hope to succeed
   b. in which I hope to succeed

10. The stadium was full of people, ____.
    a. most of whom supported Brazil
    b. most of which supported Brazil

3 Circle the best words below to complete the article.

Earthquake!

Ten minutes after the earthquake struck, the ____ (1.) ran into the remains of the building, which was located close to a ____ (2.). They were there to ____ (3.). Again and again they removed huge chunks of brick and carried the injured people ____ (4.). They didn't normally deal with ____ (5.) like earthquakes. The dangers they ____ (6.) were usually due to human error — people getting trapped in elevators and things like that — but it didn't ____ (7.) to them. Lives were lives. When it seemed as if there was no more to be done, one of the men sensed a movement, something almost ____ (8.) the human eye. They had combed every inch of the building, but the man's ____ (9.) going in there. Within minutes he emerged carrying a tiny cat. The cat's ____ (10.) had told it to hide under a cupboard, where it had subsequently become trapped.

1. a. rescuing team
   b. rescue squad
   c. rescue team

2. a. tourist site
   b. touristic area
   c. tourism site

3. a. safe lives
   b. be saved lives
   c. save lives

4. a. safely
   b. to safety
   c. for safety

5. a. nature disasters
   b. nature's disasters
   c. natural disasters

6. a. faced
   b. touched
   c. made

7. a. make the difference
   b. mean any difference
   c. make any difference

8. a. invisible to
   b. invisible for
   c. invisible with

9. a. heart was decided on
   b. heart was set on
   c. head was set on

10. a. animal's instinct
    b. intelligent instincts
    c. animal instincts

4 Finish the words to complete each sentence.

1. We found that a large m_____ of people (nearly 90%) wanted to change their job.

2. V_____ none (0.3 %) of the people felt that they would be in the same job for the rest of their lives.

3. A small m_____ (around 3%) said they had applied for a new job in the last month.

4. As f_____ as 13% of participants claimed that they would like to go (back) to school.

5. Most of the participants had been in work for ap_____ ten to fifteen years.

6. 30% said their salary is w_____ u_____ what they deserve, and want more money.

7. 60% believe they will be in their current job for a mi_____ of two more years.

5a Match the beginning of the sentence with its end.

____ 1. It's in   a. wide range of colors.
____ 2. It's as   b. by hand.
____ 3. It's the   c. of-the-art.
____ 4. It's state-   d. new.
____ 5. It's on   e. of a kind.
____ 6. It's made   f. the market.
____ 7. It's one   g. wear and tear.
____ 8. It has some   h. good as new.
____ 9. It comes in a   i. latest model.
____ 10. It's brand   j. excellent condition.

b Find expressions in Exercise 5a that mean:

1. You can choose from a selection.

   _____

2. It's handcrafted.

   _____

3. It's still in the original package.

   _____

4. It's unique.

   _____

5. It's available now.

   _____

6a Put the words in the correct order to make sentences.

____ 1. breaking/up/tricky/a/fight/can/dog/very/be

   _____

____ 2. if/hit/will/it/you/you/dog,/attack/the

   _____

____ 3. the/next/to/do/walk/dog/is/to/thing/you/the/backwards/have

   _____

____ 4. finally,/from/the/away/dogs/other/each/tie

   _____

____ 5. second,/help/get

   _____

____ 6. first,/hit/dog/the/don't

   _____

____ 7. once/you/dog's/the/help,/grab/hind/legs/have

   _____

b Number the sentences in the correct order.

Communication

1a Read the interview on the right and choose the best summary.

The interview describes ____ .

a. problems we will have in the future and possible technological solutions

b. some new inventions that may help people in the future

c. ways in which technology has improved the lives of ordinary people

b Read the interview again. Mark the statements true (*T*) or false (*F*).

____ 1. V2V involves cars "talking to each other" through a computer system.

____ 2. The new cell phone will tell you how nervous or confident you look.

____ 3. The new cell phone was invented to help people during "speed dates."

____ 4. The memory device is not just one machine.

____ 5. According to Gordon Bell, recording your life is rather boring.

c Write the words from the box in the correct category.

squeaky	gadget	unintelligible
gizmo	swerve	hand-held device
sensor	pedal	backseat driver
		steering wheel

driving	
technology	
the voice	

Future world

A: What do you have for us, Barry?

B: Well, we have an amazing selection of gadgets and gizmos for the future, including a car that can't crash, and a cell phone that tells you "you're never going to get a date if you talk like that!" And some software that will allow you to carry years and years of memories in your pocket. How about that?

A: Sounds terrifying.

B: It isn't.

A: So, tell us about the car. What is it and how does it work?

B: We're entering James Bond territory here. The system is called V2V. It stands for "vehicle to vehicle communication." Basically, we're talking about sensors on the side of the road that will exchange information with your car about what other cars are doing. Not only that, but the car will also swerve to avoid a crash. We're talking about a backseat driver, but one that's always right!

A: That's great. Sounds like a lifesaver.

B: It is. They're even working on steering wheels that can shake sleepy drivers awake and pedals that vibrate.

A: Fantastic. What about the cell phone?

B: Well, this is a different kind of lifesaver. It's going to be a big help to shy young men trying to get a date.

A: How's that?

B: It's a socially-aware cell phone that can analyze voice patterns and tell you if you sound nervous or cool. It can tell you if you're speaking too fast, or if you're unintelligible, or even if your voice is too squeaky! It was recently piloted at a speed dating session and the participants loved it!

A: Very interesting. What about the memory device?

B: It's actually a few devices: a mini-camera that can fit into a contact lens and a microphone that fits in your ear. You download the data onto a hand-held device and there you have it: a lifetime's worth of memories.

A: But who would want it?

B: Gordon Bell.

A: Who's he?

B: A researcher who's been recording his entire life, since 1998, for a project called MyLifeBits.

A: Wow.

B: He scans all of his photos and documents, and records meetings, phone calls and emails, and he wears a mini-camera round his neck to get an image of everything he sees.

A: But isn't it unbelievably boring?

B: Well, according to Bell, it's not. He says it's similar to having an assistant with a perfect memory. But I imagine it depends on just how boring your life is.

Vocabulary

2 Complete the paragraphs with words from the box.

> overrated   waste   live
> underrated   benefits

In my view, cell phones are _____ (**1.**). They are not a complete _____ (**2.**) of space, but we don't really need them. In the past, we just made arrangements more carefully or used pay phones.

We can't _____ (**3.**) without cell phones. They have huge _____ (**4.**) for society because they allow us to communicate more, which is a great thing. I actually think they are _____ (**5.**); we don't realize how useful cell phones are until we find ourselves in an emergency.

Grammar

3 Circle the correct words or phrases to complete the sentences. Two choices may be possible.

1. She _____ to college, but he just wanted to find a job.
   a. insisted Ben going
   b. encouraged Ben to go
   c. suggested that Ben go
2. Morger _____ the money.
   a. warned us to steal
   b. denied stealing
   c. threatened to steal
3. Claudia _____ eating the cake, even though I was innocent.
   a. accused me of
   b. threatened to
   c. blamed me for
4. I _____ I had been stupid.
   a. admitted that
   b. confessed that
   c. informed that
5. Ling _____ take our warm clothes.
   a. encouraged that we
   b. told us to
   c. reminded us to
6. He always _____ his record was the best.
   a. accused that
   b. maintained that
   c. insisted on

4 Rewrite each sentence using the correct form of the verb in parentheses.

1. Mr. Anderson told us again to read the safety precautions. (remind)
   Mr. Anderson _____.
2. "My advice is to call a doctor," said Lena. (suggest)
   Lena _____.
3. We had taken it for granted that you knew each other. (assume)
   We _____.
4. She said Tom had stolen the apple. (accuse)
   She _____.
5. We had to say that we didn't know the answer. (admit)
   We _____.
6. I said "well done" to her for passing her exam. (congratulate)
   I _____.
7. Dad said he'd withhold our allowance if we continue to behave badly. (threaten)
   Dad _____.
8. "I've never met her before!" said Young-soo. (deny)
   Young-soo _____.

5 First put the letters in parentheses in the correct order to make a word. Then, put the words in the correct order to anwer the question.

1. **A:** So, what will you do next?
   B: (nusqoiet) _____/a/that's/good

   _____
2. **A:** Which of your co-stars was your favorite?
   B: (lelw), _____/I/of/all/them/loved

   _____
3. **A:** Of all your movies, which would you like to be remembered for?
   B: (tel) _____/see/me

   _____
4. **A:** Do you regret starring in any of your movies?
   B: (ikhnt) _____/I'd/that/about/to/have

   _____
5. **A:** Will you get married again for a sixth time?
   B: (rkctyi) _____/that's

   _____
6. **A:** Who was your favorite director?
   B: (iitfcldfu) _____/question/that's/a

   _____

Vocabulary

1 Complete the sentences with words from the box.

> security   out   hair   buzz   and

1. Because of stress and high expectations, many tennis players burn _____ before they reach 30.

2. A lot of business people who are already rich and successful say that the main motivator is no longer money, but the _____ and excitement of making deals.

3. Mark was tearing his _____ out with frustration when they overlooked him for a promotion again.

4. Julie tries to save some money every week as a _____ blanket in case of unexpected disasters!

5. I don't think work should come before family; your career isn't the be-all _____ end-all.

Grammar

2 Match the questions to the answers.

_____ 1. Why did she look so sad?

_____ 2. Why did they look tired?

_____ 3. Why are they such a mess?

_____ 4. Why did the police stop him?

_____ 5. What were all those people doing there?

_____ 6. When did Brian start his trip?

_____ 7. Why isn't Anna Rita taking the class?

_____ 8. What were all those secret meetings about?

_____ 9. Why didn't Suyin answer the phone?

_____ 10. What's she doing in that room?

a. They were being taken on a tour of the harbor.

b. They'd been talking all night.

c. They'd been thinking of selling the company.

d. I think she's been playing computer games all evening.

e. She may have been sleeping when you called.

f. He'll have been traveling for exactly two weeks this time tomorrow.

g. He must have been driving too fast.

h. She was going to a funeral.

i. She's expecting a baby in one month!

j. They've been painting the window frames.

3 Complete the story using the correct form of the verbs in parentheses. Use the continuous form of the verb if possible.

My 92-year-old great aunt is called "Dutchie," but that's just a family nickname. My grandmother says that Dutchie's real name is Adulcia—or at least that's what she thinks. My grandmother says that she never heard her sister called by her real name, so she's not even sure how to pronounce it. As a child, my great aunt could never pronounce it either, and her attempts always sounded like "Dutchie," so the name stuck.

Dutchie _____ (**1.** live) with us in New York City right now. She has never been in a big city before. In fact, until this year she _____ (**2.** never/be) more than 50 miles from the small town in Vermont where she was born. However, even though she had seen very little of the world, she _____ (**3.** gather) a lot of wisdom throughout her life.

My great aunt and I have always been close. I lived with her the summer after I graduated from college. I'll always remember our first morning together that summer. When I woke up, it _____ (**4.** rain) hard. I felt as bad as the weather outside. At that time, I _____ (**5.** have) a lot of problems with my parents, who wanted me to attend medical school. I _____ (**6.** struggle) to convince them that I wasn't cut out to be a doctor. The sight of blood actually made me ill and I _____ (**7.** hate) studying. Dutchie _____ (**8.** sense) right away that something was wrong. We had a long talk that morning, as the rain lashed the windows and drummed on the roof. Dutchie took my hands in hers and looked deep into my eyes. Her advice to me was simple: "Choose a job that you love, and you'll never work a day in your life." I've _____ (**9.** follow) her advice for over 30 years, and I've never regretted it.

Reading

4a Read the ideas. Check them once if you already do them. Check twice if you would like to try them.

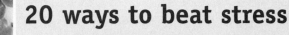

20 ways to beat stress

____ 1. **Learn something new, such as a sport, a language, or a skill, like painting. Short bursts of intense concentration are a great way to relieve stress.**

____ 2. Teach yourself massage techniques, yoga, or t'ai chi.

____ 3. **Make the most of seasonal fruits, such as strawberries, raspberries and cherries. They are full of feel-good nutrients.**

____ 4. Pamper yourself once a week: watch a movie, have a soothing bath with oils, or buy yourself a bouquet of your favorite flowers.

____ 5. **Write down something good that happened to you in each year of your life.**

____ 6. Avoid sugary snacks and sodas that are likely to give you a temporary high. Drink water and snack on natural foods, such as nuts, instead.

____ 7. **Call up your inner child, and do something you haven't done for years, like playing on a swing or putting on an old pair of roller skates.**

____ 8. Talk to someone about your problems. Bottling things up only makes them worse.

____ 9. **If you have a sedentary job, do something physical like gardening or going for a run.**

____ 10. Switch off every machine in the house, ignore all but the most urgent emails for 24 hours, get comfortable, and read a book.

____ 11. **Bake bread. Kneading dough is hard work, but soothing, and the smell of fresh bread is guaranteed to lift your spirits.**

____ 12. Get back to nature. Treat yourself to a long walk in a park.

____ 13. **Meditate. Cultivate optimistic thoughts. Think of what you have, not what you want.**

____ 14. Get rid of all the clutter on your desk. Throw away everything you don't really need.

____ 15. **Look through your wardrobe. If you haven't worn something for over 18 months, give it to a charity, or to someone who will wear it.**

____ 16. Go to a karaoke bar and sing away your worries. Alternatively, close all the doors, put on your favorite music at full volume, and sing or dance until you're exhausted.

____ 17. **Go to bed an hour earlier than usual to improve your sleep.**

____ 18. Cut down on alcohol, nicotine, and caffeine. Reduce your intake gradually, and you may find that you can give it up altogether.

____ 19. **Go home a different way. For instance, walk home from work if it's not too far.**

____ 20. Eat at least one meal a day with friends or family.

b Find words in the article that mean:

1. sudden periods of activity or noise (*n.*) (suggestion 1) _____

2. give someone lots of loving care and attention (e.g., buy them gifts, etc.) (*v.*) (suggestion 4) _____

3. makes you feel calm and less worried (*adj.*) (suggestion 4) _____

4. a feeling of having lots of energy or great happiness (*n.*) (suggestion 6) _____

5. not allow yourself to show feelings (*v. + prep.*) (suggestion 8) _____

6. involving sitting down and not moving (*adj.*) (suggestion 9) _____

7. work hard to help something grow (*v.*) (suggestion 13) _____

8. things that fill space untidily and aren't necessary (*n.*) (suggestion 14) _____

c Complete the sentences using the correct form of the words in Exercise 4b.

1. I hated my _____ lifestyle, stuck behind a desk for eight hours a day, so I took up jogging.

2. Loretta went for a _____ massage every morning.

3. Don't _____ your problems. Tell me about them.

4. We need to remove useless _____ from our lives and to focus on what is essential.

5. My husband really _____ me. He buys me flowers and new clothes every week.

6. She's very good at _____ personal relationships. She writes letters, invites people to dinner, and always keeps in touch.

7. Caffeine gives you a temporary _____, but you shouldn't have too much of it.

8. I completed all my work in a two-day _____ of energy!

Communication

1 Read five phone messages. For each message, answer the following questions. Use a separate sheet of paper.

 a. What exactly is the problem?

 b. What must the receiver of the message do?

Message 1

Hi Joseph, it's Chris. Just wanted to say that something's come up and, basically, I'm not going to be able to make it to your place by six, so I'll try and get there, well, as soon as I can. It's a problem with the air conditioning here at the office, and basically the only time the maintenance guy can come is after 5:30, so I have to stay a few minutes late. Anyway, I'll be there as soon as possible. Bye.

Message 2

Hello, it's Sandy from Small World Travel. There's a problem with your tickets to Fiji. Can you give me a call at (555) 249-0312. Thank you.

Message 3

Hello, honey, it's me. If you get this message, can you try and get in touch with Monica about babysitting? I completely forgot to ask her yesterday, and I don't have her phone number on me. We need her from about seven until twelve tomorrow. Talk to you later.

Message 4

Hello. My name is Alexandra Duvall, and I bought a Classic Body Toner Home Gym from you on Saturday. It was delivered on Monday, but there seems to be a problem with it. Right now, I can't get the machine to work at all, even though the guys who delivered it said it was easy, and I've followed the instructions in the manual. Could you please send a mechanic over as soon as possible—I really need to get it working immediately. My customer order number is 675637. Thank you.

Message 5

James, this is Liz Jordan. I just got the message that our keynote speaker is sick and won't be able to come to the conference, so it's pretty urgent that we find a replacement. I haven't talked to William yet, so could you please pass on this message. And give me a call. You can reach me on my cell any time. Bye.

Grammar

2 Circle the correct choice.

http://www.great_advice.com/marriageconcerns.html

Great_advice.com

My fiancée and I are planning our wedding. The *matter/ worrying/thing* (**1.**) is, we want a small, informal one (family and best friends only), but we don't want to offend people by not inviting them. The fact *to the matter/remains/of the matter* (**2.**) is, they all invited us to their weddings, and we feel a little bit mean having a private one. **Alex**

Alex, I understand your concerns, but the *matter/point/ trouble* (**3.**) is, it's your special day, and it's for you to decide how you want to spend it. Ignore all other considerations. **Sajid**

Hi, Alex, one *thing you could/option you/way to* (**4.**) do is organize a party for all your friends a few weeks before you get married, and explain to them that you want a quiet wedding. **Sue**

http://www.happy_to_help.com/marriageconcerns.html

Happy_to_help.com 😊

My husband's son from his first marriage still lives at home, although he is 23. *The thing irritates/The matter for/What irritates* (**5.**) me is that he doesn't work or study, and he does nothing around the house, treating me like a servant. My husband keeps saying "give him time," but my patience is running out. *What we need/What needs/The matter* (**6.**) to do is talk to him seriously about the situation, but my husband refuses. **Georgia**

Dear Georgia, although your husband's attitude is, in some ways, understandable, the fact *stays/remains that/ remains* (**7.**) he needs to take the lead in this situation. He must talk to the boy. **Kerry**

Georgia, *what could happen/what you could try/the trouble* (**8.**) is to set some rules about housework; and draw up a schedule that everyone has to follow. **Joanne**

Vocabulary

3 Circle the correct choices to complete the article.

As anyone who's ever waited in a long line will testify, there's nothing like bad service to kill a business. It can also be a _major source/big root/serious consequence_ (**1.**) of stress when something goes wrong and no one seems willing to help. We've heard stories of people waiting on the phone for an hour before customer service picks up, or people hanging on for weeks to get faulty equipment replaced. The _stem/result/cause_ (**2.**) is that customers will go elsewhere next time, and also tell others their horror stories. Mark Bradley wrote a book called _Inconvenience Stores_ about a year of customer service in the UK. The idea _had it origins in/was originated in/was original in_ (**3.**) some research Bradley was doing for a business presentation, but the fascinating anecdotes _result in/had a result that/resulted_

_in_ (**4.**) increased interest, and eventually he wrote a whole book. It doesn't make for happy reading. At one point, he asks for a latte and is told "You'll have to go to Leeds (another city) for that." He concludes that much of the poor service _has its origins/origins/gives rise_ (**5.**) in the fact that employees have no power to make decisions. In one hotel chain, employees have to get permission to say no to customers. Naturally, this _consequences/causes of/leads to_ (**6.**) serious problems for the hotel. So, how can businesses _reach/bring about/breed_ (**7.**) change in the form of better service? Bradley thinks that companies need to improve morale among employees and give them the freedom to do what's right for the customer. The _source/consequences/origins_ (**8.**) could be wonderful for us all!

---

4 Complete the conversations by adding words from the box.

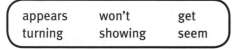

appears	won't	get
turning	showing	seem

1. **A:** I'm having problems on the oven.
   B: Yes, there's something wrong with it.
2. **A:** I can't ___ the washing machine to wash the clothes.
   B: That's because it's a dryer!
3. **A:** The computer doesn't ___ to be working.
   B: That's because you haven't turned it on.
4. **A:** The car still ___ start.
   B: Let's call the mechanic.
5. **A:** The clock is always ___ the wrong time.
   B: I know. It needs a new battery.
6. **A:** This light ___ to be broken. It doesn't turn on.
   B: I think the bulb's burned out.

Writing

5a Read the opening lines of this essay. Number the sentences in the correct order to complete the essay.

> Procrastination affects most of us at some time or another. <u>For this reason</u>, a number of studies have been carried out looking into its causes and consequences. <u>Furthermore</u>, we have tried to develop and evaluate a number of possible solutions to the problem.

____ Consequently, putting it off just adds to that feeling of anxiety, because time is running out.

__1__ The first cause we discovered was a lack of concentration.

____ For example, some perfectionists believe they must do extensive research before writing anything.

____ Instead of dealing with the task at hand, many people let their mind wander, staring out of the window or surfing the net.

____ This means that they read and read but never actually get around to writing the paper.

____ A third cause is perfectionism.

____ The second cause was fear; when we are worried that a task is beyond us, we tend to put it off.

b Underline useful linking and sequencing expressions. The first two have been done.

1a Read the excerpt from a story. Which person was most frightened? _____

"Don't go in there," said June. But they were determined to go. Mike, the oldest, said, "Why should we listen to you anyway? You're just a kid!"

"It's haunted!" replied June. "And if you go in there, I'll tell my mother!" Mike just laughed and said, "You're lying." But Sally was nervous.

"What if June's right?" she asked. Mike said, "Don't be ridiculous. Ghosts don't exist. We'll be out of there in two minutes."

"OK," said Sally. As they approached the house, June ran the other way and shouted, "Don't forget what happened to the dog!"

"Thanks!" said Mike, as he grabbed Sally's hand and stepped through the doorway. At that moment, their lives changed, and nothing would ever be the same again.

b Read the excerpt again and complete the sentences. Use the words in parentheses when they are given.

1. June warned _____.
   (the house)
2. June claimed _____.
3. June threatened _____.
4. Mike accused _____.
5. Mike informed _____.
   (ghosts)
6. Mike persuaded _____.
   (go in)
7. Sally agreed _____.
   (the house)
8. June reminded _____.

2 Circle the correct words or phrases to complete the sentences.

1. The book is not nearly as interesting as I thought it would be. It's a little ____.
   a. underrated   c. indispensable
   b. overrated
2. The new banking laws have ____.
   a. had big benefits for us   c. benefit us
   b. made big benefits for us
3. All this technology isn't really necessary. We ____.
   a. can't do without it   c. can do without it
   b. can do without
4. That building is hideous, and it serves no purpose. What ____!
   a. a space waste   c. a waster of space
   b. a waste of space

3 Match the beginning of each sentence with its end.

1. ___ 1. We've built a tree house, which
   ___ 2. We've been building a tree house, which
   a. we're hoping to finish tomorrow.
   b. the children play in every day.

2. ___ 1. He might have been voting
   ___ 2. He might have voted
   a. this morning, which would explain why he wasn't here.
   b. for an independent candidate in the last election, but I doubt it.

3. ___ 1. Dana was being taught Chinese
   ___ 2. Dana was taught Chinese
   a. the last time I saw her.
   b. when she was a child.

4. ___ 1. We'll have been studying
   ___ 2. We'll have studied
   a. this verb form six times if we do this lesson.
   b. here for exactly two years by this time on Monday.

5. ___ 1. It's raining
   ___ 2. It rains
   a. between June and September.
   b. again.

6. ___ 1. I've been seeing her
   ___ 2. I've seen her
   a. in the same place, at the same convention, every year since 1982!
   b. before.

4 Seven of these items have an extra word. Cross out the extra words and check the correct sentences.

1. Behaviorist theory has its own roots in an experiment by Ivan Pavlov. _____

2. His research was to have far-reaching and consequences for psychology. _____

3. When Pavlov placed meat powder on a dog's tongue, the dog salivated. _____

4. Pavlov then began ringing a bell just before giving the dog the meat powder. _____

5. This resulted but in the dog salivating when it heard the bell, even if it _____

6. didn't get any meat powder afterwards. Many psychologists concluded that by _____

7. a major source of motivation is conditioning. This had a huge influence so _____

8. on many areas of life, including language learning. For example, _____

9. behaviorist theory gave a rise to the audiolingual method (listen and repeat). _____

10. It also brought us about many changes in the teaching materials used. _____

5 Rewrite each sentence using the words in parentheses.

1. I'm fed up with all that noise. (thing/irritates)

   _____

   _____

2. My main concern is the cost involved. (what/worries)

   _____

   _____

3. To tell the truth, I'm tired of this game. (fact)

   _____

   _____

4. There are too many people; that's the problem. (trouble/is)

   _____

   _____

5. He broke his promise. There's nothing we can do to change that. (fact/remains)

   _____

   _____

6. The house is in good condition. That's the important thing. (point/is)

   _____

   _____

6 Each conversation has one mistake. Find the mistakes and correct them.

1. **A:** This toaster keeps to burn the toast.

   B: Well, why don't you buy a new one?

2. **A:** I can't get this door to close. Can you help me?

   B: Let me to see.

3. **A:** Can you give me a hand tomorrow? I'm having problems finishing all this work.

   B: I'll have to think of that. I'm pretty busy myself.

4. **A:** My car can't start. What can I do?

   B: That's a difficult question.

5. **A:** This drawer seems to be too stuck. How does it open?

   B: That's a good question.

UNIT 9
People with vision

LESSON 1

Vocabulary

1 Complete the puzzle and find the key word.

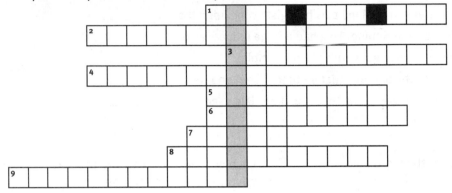

1. It was funny to watch although the acting was really ____.
2. The Mona Lisa is a ____.
3. It was a beautiful opera and the scenery was just ____.
4. The town is full of ____ architecture.
5. The artist's ____ of the royal family are well-known.
6. The special effects in the new *Star Wars* movie are ____.
7. It's a long book about the history of nuclear physics, so it's a very ____ read.
8. Unfortunately, the characters are rather ____.
9. I'm really into ____ art these days.

Grammar

2 Circle the correct prepositions. Who is the artist?

Perhaps one of the most tragic masters of art, this painter yearned *for/on/to* (**1.**) recognition during his lifetime, but was denied it until after his death. He is universally seen as one of the greatest artists *at/in/of* (**2.**) all time.

To/On/For (**3.**) one occasion, he said of his paintings: "I cannot help it if my paintings do not sell. But the time will come when people will realize that they are worth more than the cost of the paint." His vision was correct. This artist was an indisputable genius, who was also undeniably ignored. He became famous *for/of/at* (**4.**) the hundreds of bold, bright paintings he produced, many of which have become some of the best known, paintings of the 20th century, but only one of which was ever sold during his lifetime. The work he specialized *at/in/on* (**5.**) was avant-garde *in/for/of* (**6.**) his time, and as such, was not accepted by the general public.

He spent the latter part of his life absorbed *in/on/at* (**7.**) his work. However, he was always *over/in/under* (**8.**) stress, and suffered *for/from/of* (**9.**) depression. It is now thought that epilepsy may have contributed *to/with/in* (**10.**) the psychological breakdowns that plagued him until his untimely death.

Reading

3a Read the biography on page 69. Then choose the correct answers.

1. Why is Stephen Hawking so famous?
   a. Because he has researched time travel.
   b. Because of his ideas and his physical condition.
   c. Because he is unable to speak.

2. Stephen suffers from a rare disease that
   a. has left him in a vegetative state.
   b. means he can talk unaided but he cannot move.
   c. makes both speech and movement almost impossible.

3. His physical condition has
   a. meant that he never enjoyed a family life.
   b. probably contributed to his fame.
   c. impeded him from achieving greatness in his professional career.

Stephen Hawking: Triumph of a Mind over Matter

(1) Stephen Hawking is undeniably one of the world's most gifted and revered scientists. His groundbreaking contributions to the study of the universe and the nature of space and time have electrified the scientific world. Moreover, his public appearances and best-selling books, in which he explains his theories to general readers, have made him an international celebrity. His achievements are even more remarkable given his severe physical handicaps: Hawking has a rare disease called amyotrophic lateral sclerosis (ALS), a condition that gradually left him almost completely paralyzed and unable to speak. The story of how Hawking overcame the limitations of his disease and continued his scientific work is nothing short of remarkable.

(2) Hawking was born in Oxford, England, on January 8, 1942, into a distinguished family. His mother had been one of the first women to be accepted to Oxford University. His father, also an Oxford graduate, was a respected medical researcher. Meals at the Hawking home were usually eaten in silence, with each member of the family engrossed in a book. After supper, the Hawkings would often lie in the backyard and gaze up at the stars. Hawking's mother recalls, "Stephen always had a strong sense of wonder. And I could see that the stars would draw him."

(3) Although he was recognized as being very intelligent, Hawking did not put much effort into his schoolwork. Instead, he busied himself with personal projects, inventing board games and building a primitive computer out of recycled parts that could solve basic math problems. Despite his lack of focus in the classroom, Hawking graduated with honors from Oxford University in 1962, with a degree in natural science, and went on to Cambridge to do research in cosmology.

(4) It was at this time that Hawking began to exhibit his first symptoms of ALS. He started to trip and fall down and had difficulty speaking clearly. After a series of tests, doctors made a grave diagnosis: the nerves controlling his muscles had begun shutting down. They predicted that Hawking would have only a couple of years to live. He refused to allow the devastating news to crush his spirit. In fact, Hawking found he began to enjoy life as never before. He asked a fellow student named Jane Wilde to marry him, and she accepted. He began to make progress with his research and won a fellowship at Gonville and Caius College, Cambridge. Hawking and Wilde married in 1965 and had three children together. As Hawking's body deteriorated, his mind soared to new heights. In 1974, he amazed the scientific community by using quantum theory and general relativity to demonstrate that black holes can emit radiation. The next year, he published his first book, *Large Scale Structure of Space Time*. In 1979, Hawking was named Lucasian Professor of Mathematics at Cambridge, a great honor for someone so young.

(5) However, Hawking's physical condition worsened. Confined to a wheelchair since 1969, he gradually lost the ability to perform basic tasks, such as feeding himself and getting in and out of bed. In 1985, pneumonia robbed him of the ability to speak. Refusing to give up his work, Hawking learned to use a speaking program that he directed with a sensor attached to his cheek muscles. It allowed him to select words on a computer screen that were then "spoken" by an electronic speech synthesizer. Using this system, Hawking wrote *A Brief History of Time* in 1988, an easy-to-understand explanation of the workings of the universe that has sold over 25 million copies worldwide. Other books and important discoveries followed and secured Hawking's reputation as the preeminent theoretical physicist in the world. Today one of the longest-lived and most productive survivors of ALS, Hawking continues to write at a prolific rate and remains dedicated to finding the answers to science's biggest mystery: the explanation of how the universe began.

b Find words or phrases in the article that mean:

_____ 1. much admired (*adj.*) (paragrah 1)

_____ 2. new and radically different (*adj.*) (paragraph 1)

_____ 3. make people very excited (*v.*) (paragraph 1)

_____ 4. completely interested in something (*v.*) (paragraph 2)

_____ 5. very simple, basic (*adj.*) (paragraph 3)

_____ 6. seriously bad (*adj.*) (paragraph 4)

_____ 7. the best of its kind (*adj.*) (paragraph 5)

c On a separate sheet of paper, rewrite this summary. Correct the mistakes.

Stephen Hawking was born in London, England in 1942. A hard-working student, Hawking spent all of his time in the classroom. Since he was a small child, Hawkins suffered from a disease known as ALS. Doctors predicted that he would only have a couple of months to live. However, Hawking refused to give up hope. He continued his research and married Jane Wilde in 1979. Hawking discovered new information about earthquakes that surprised the scientific world. His first book, *A Brief History of Time*, was published in 1988. These and other accomplishments have cemented his reputation as one of the greatest scientists of all time.

Vocabulary

1   Put the letters in parentheses in the correct order to make words to complete the sentences.

1. I like _____ paintings best, especially ones by artists like Kandinsky and Mirò. (scatbart)

2. It's very _____. You can't help but notice it when you walk into the room. (tigrnski)

3. His techniques were very _____ for the time. (navat-draeg)

4. Her still life paintings are _____ and simple. (lacm)

5. The landscapes are very _____ and relaxing to look at. (nailqurt)

6. He is famous for his _____ portraits. (lorcoluf)

7. I found the sculptures of dead animals highly _____. (tirgsubind)

8. It's a masterpiece. Absolutely _____! (racpeslatcu)

9. Their earlier works were more _____ in style. (ladanotirit)

10. Some people love them, but personally I find landscapes a little _____. (ludl)

2   Complete the conversations by adding words from the box.

> admired   my   into   relate
> all-time   fan   cup   kind

1. **A:** Did you like the dress?
   B: I'm sorry, it's just not my of thing at all.

2. **A:** What do you think of the decor?
   B: It's really not taste.

3. **A:** Did you enjoy Seiko's latest exhibition?
   B: Yes. I'm really her work.

4. **A:** How about this one? Do you like the style?
   B: It's not really my of tea.

5. **A:** Have you heard the new Rihanna album?
   B: I'm not a big of her stuff.

6. **A:** *Twilight* is on TV tonight.
   B: Great. It's an favorite of mine.

7. **A:** Ali Smith won an award for her latest novel.
   B: She deserved to. I've always her work.

8. **A:** What do you think of the exhibition?
   B: I just can't to this kind of thing.

Grammar

3   Use the words in parentheses to complete the sentences.

Ex: _As I was saying_, I'm going to talk to you about education.

1. I can _____ see what you mean. (sort)

2. _____, I haven't really understood what you are talking about. (honest)

3. _____, I would rather stay at home and watch a movie. (truth)

4. We can _____ be sure that they intend to buy. (more)

5. _____, we should be able to get a good price. (rate)

6. _____, I wouldn't want to stay there on my own. (mind)

7. _____, I think the ideas should be discussed at a meeting. (matter, fact)

8. _____, it is the best offer we are going to get. (far, concerned)

9. _____ when we should leave, I don't think it makes any difference. (for)

10. _____, they proved us wrong in the end. (fact)

11. _____ changing the policy completely, I'm not in a position to answer. (regarding)

Vocabulary

4   Complete the sentences with words from the box.

> hideout   undercover   stuffed   haul
> tracked   mastermind   chainsaw   crack

1. He is suspected of being the _____ behind the bombings.

2. The man was discovered in a _____ in the woods.

3. He worked _____ in Colombia and Panama.

4. Detectives finally _____ her down in California.

5. She quickly _____ two more sweaters into her bag.

6. They used a _____ to cut through the heavy doors.

7. This new evidence could help detectives to _____ the case.

8. The gang escaped with a _____ worth hundreds of dollars.

Reading

5a Read the article and choose the best title.

    a. A Good Deal   **b.** Momentarily Fooled   **c.** Texan Rebel

(1) In 1952, Elmyr de Hory returned to Los Angeles after a prosperous sojourn in Dallas, Texas. He had managed to sell some of his stash of alleged masterpieces, including some Picasso and Matisse drawings. He had made a huge profit and was hoping he would be equally successful in Southern California. Elmyr had set up an appointment with art dealer Frank Perls, owner of a well-known Beverly Hills gallery, and he planned to unload more of his artwork for another sizeable profit.

(2) Elmyr dressed in his best suit for the occasion, carrying with him a large portfolio. At his meeting with Perls, Elmyr presented what he claimed were drawings he'd inherited from his family following World War II. The portfolio purportedly included sketches from Picasso, Matisse, Renoir and Modigliani.

(3) Perls took one look at the work and was immensely impressed. After all, it's not often that one has the chance to hold great masterpieces by some of the world's most famous artists. However, the longer Perls looked at the pictures, the more concerned he became. It was clear that something was wrong, and Perls' worrisome expression discomforted Elmyr.

(4) According to Clifford Irving's book, *Fake!*, Perls questioned Elmyr about his address and other detailed personal information, causing Elmyr to become nervous. Perls then calmly placed the pictures back into the portfolio, tied the strings, and then suddenly threw them at Elmyr. Elmyr was shocked by the unexpected action, and was uncertain what to do next, until Perls ordered him to get out.

(5) Elmyr then walked out of the gallery with Perls yelling behind him. Perls observed what an untrained eye would likely never notice: these works were fakes. It was also true that they were created masterfully.

(6) To Perls' surprise, Elmyr asked him, after being thrown out of the gallery, whether he thought the drawings were well done. According to Irving, Perls replied: "They certainly fooled me for a few minutes," before ordering the counterfeiter away again. The incident was not Elmyr's first or last time at trying to sell excellent forgeries. In fact, he had been doing it successfully for years.

(7) Unbeknownst to Frank Perls, Elmyr had sold some forgeries to Perls' brother, Klaus, in New York several years earlier. Elmyr's involvement with the two Perls brothers would later cause unexpected problems. In fact, one of the Perls brothers would be directly involved in what would later be the end of Elmyr's career as a skillful art forger.

(8) For approximately three decades, Elmyr de Hory used his extraordinary talent to reproduce masterpieces from some of the world's greatest artists, including Picasso, Vlaminck, Chagall, Toulouse-Lautrec, Dufy, Derain, Matisse, Degas, Bonnard, Laurencin, and Modigliani. His accuracy for detail fooled even the most skilled art connoisseurs into believing that his creations were authentic. Given their alleged provenance, Elmyr sold his forgeries for high prices. Moreover, he managed to elude Interpol and the FBI for most of his criminal career.

(9) Elmyr de Hory eventually became known worldwide as one of the most talented art forgers in history. Even after his death, Elmyr's works still attracted attention. Some of them even sold for the same prices as the originals. Like many famous painters, however, he died penniless, after a series of unfortunate events.

b Read the article again. Mark the statements true (*T*) or false (*F*).

_____ **1.** Elmyr de Hory traveled to Dallas with just a couple of paintings.

_____ **2.** He sold paintings for a small profit to art dealers.

_____ **3.** Perls immediately spotted Elmyr as a fake by the way he was dressed.

_____ **4.** Elmyr made up stories about the origins of the paintings.

_____ **5.** Perls' questions worried Elmyr.

_____ **6.** Elmyr had been successfully selling fake paintings for about 30 years.

_____ **7.** He had been chased constantly by the FBI and Interpol.

c Figure out the meaning of the words. Use the context of the article to help you.

    1. prosperous (paragraph 1) _____

    2. stash (paragraph 1) _____

    3. purportedly (paragraph 2) _____

    4. worrisome (paragraph 3) _____

    5. masterfully (paragraph 5) _____

    6. forgeries (paragraph 7) _____

    7. fooled (paragraph 8) _____

    8. elude (paragraph 8) _____

Vocabulary

1 Complete the conversation with words from the box.

> out of focus   disposable   close-up
> foreground   accessories   flash
> vacation shots   digital

Julia: Do you want to come and see my _____ (1.) of Thailand?

Kasem: Sure.

Julia: That's me in the _____ (2.). Behind me is the Royal Palace. This one's a little _____ (3.). You can't see it very clearly.

Kasem: But most of these are great pictures. Did you use a _____ (4.) camera?

Julia: No, just a cheap little _____ (5.) camera. I threw it away after the vacation.

Kasem: So it didn't have any _____ (6.) like a tripod or anything?

Julia: No way! I prefer to keep it simple. This one's a little dark. We took it at night and I don't think the _____ (7.) was working.

Kasem: Wow! Who's this, taking up the whole frame?!

Julia: This is a _____ (8.) of my aunt. You can see every pore in her skin!

Grammar

2 Match the beginning of the sentence with its end.

_____ 1. I wish I hadn't
_____ 2. I wish I
_____ 3. If only they
_____ 4. It's about
_____ 5. It's high time
_____ 6. I'd rather you didn't put
_____ 7. What if you hadn't
_____ 8. Suppose I could

a. time you got a haircut.
b. your feet on the furniture.
c. been wearing a seat belt?
d. were here now.
e. offer you a bonus?
f. we had a little talk.
g. bought that car.
h. could play the guitar.

3 Rewrite each sentence using the word in parentheses.

1. Rashid lost his passport, so he couldn't board the plane. (only)
   If _____.

2. You're acting like a child and you should stop! (high)
   It's _____.

3. We really should get back to work now. (about)
   It's _____ _____.

4. Can you imagine being offered that job? Would you accept? (if)
   What _____?

5. What will happen if we press this button? (suppose)
   _____?

6. Lucia is an only child, but she wants a baby sister. (wish)
   Lucia _____.

7. What did you want to do last night: go out or watch a DVD? (rather)
   Would _____?

4 On a separate sheet of paper, put the words in the correct order to answer the questions.

1. What if the board asked you to become chairman of the company?
   it's/agree/highly/I'd/likely

2. Suppose they stopped you illegally? What would you do?
   I/taking/consider/them/court/definitely/to/would

3. If she asked you, would you lend her ten thousand dollars?
   it's/to/I'd/able/be/that/do/unlikely/that

4. You're not thinking of dropping out of the class, are you?
   there's/I/do/way/that/would/no

5. What if we offered you half of our winnings?
   I/agree/probably/that/to/would

6. Would you be willing to coach the team for free?
   I/that/I/might/suppose/doing/consider

Communication

5a Read the interview with a photographer. Answer the questions on a separate sheet of paper.

   1. How did her family influence her choice of career?

   2. What did she like about her first camera?

   3. Why does she take different types of photos?

   4. What type of pictures is she taking these days?

   5. What "has its own sort of visual vocabulary" and what do you think she means by this?

b Complete the summary. Read the interview again to check your answers.

> Sandrine started by taking photos of _____ (1.) in her _____ (2.) garden at the age of _____ (3.). She now photographs many things, including nature and famous _____ _____ (4.). She thinks a photographer's job is to capture _____ (5.) and _____ (6.). She says she is interested in _____ (7.). Sandrine lives near a _____ (8.) and loves to photograph the light there.

c Find the phrases in the interview. Match them to the definitions.

   ____ **1.** what distinguishes you from

   ____ **2.** your incredibly diverse output

   ____ **3.** a restless soul

   ____ **4.** being pigeonholed

   ____ **5.** feeling a little bit peeved

   ____ **6.** at the end of the lens

   ____ **7.** every subject under the sun

   ____ **8.** a sense of awe

a. as the subject of a photo

b. being forced to fit into a category

c. what makes you different

d. all the topics that exist

e. a feeling of wonder because something is amazing or beyond normal life

f. someone who can't stay still or stay in the same place

g. feeling annoyed

h. the things you produce that are in a very wide range of styles

A PHOTOGRAPHER'S MEMORIES

I: Sandrine, can you tell us a bit about how you got started as a photographer?

S: It all goes back to my grandmother, actually. She lived in Colombia as a child, and when she moved back to West Virginia, she insisted on planting tropical flowers in this tiny back garden of hers because they reminded her of her childhood. Whenever the flowers bloomed, the colors were astonishing. On my tenth birthday, my father gave me a Polaroid camera and I started taking pictures of grandma's garden. And the beauty of the Polaroid was that you didn't have to send the pictures away to be developed. They just slipped out of the bottom of the camera in all their glory.

I: From pictures of grandma's garden to celebrities, landscapes, underwater photography, and even social realism. What distinguishes you from other photographers is your incredibly diverse output. The product of a restless soul, perhaps?

S: You could say that. I dislike being pigeonholed. I remember reading an article about contemporary photographers a few years ago, which described me as "Sandrine Kafer, the celebrity photographer," and I remember feeling a little bit peeved that that was how some journalist saw me. I'd always thought of myself as a photographer pure and simple, whose job is to capture a moment of truth and beauty. Whether it's a famous person at the end of the lens, or two little boys on a bicycle, or soldiers, or life at the bottom of the ocean, in many ways it's the same thing to me.

I: So this diversity hasn't been a conscious career decision?

S: Not really, no. I just take opportunities where I find them, and I suppose, above all, I'm interested in everything. I have a library of about 6,000 books at home, very few of them on photography, and they cover every subject under the sun. And once you start getting interested in something, you want to see it and find the truth in it, and then, of course, if you're a photographer, you want to capture it on film.

I: Your recent work seems less crowded, perhaps more tranquil than anything you've done before.

S: Well, I live on 20 acres of land with a river close by, and birds and animals. The light is stunning, and it always amazes me that the river can look like this at five in the morning, and like that at midday, and different again at dusk. Actually, whenever you work with water, there is a sense of awe. It's where life began. It has its own rhythm and its own sort of visual vocabulary.

1a Add the correct prepositions.

1. devoted his life _____
2. the development _____
3. _____ the field (e.g., of physics)
4. be famous _____ (something)
5. immersed _____
6. specializes _____
7. succeed _____
8. _____ several occasions
9. in recognition _____
10. draw inspiration _____
11. (one of the best) _____ all time

b On a separate sheet of paper, rewrite the sentences that contain phrases in bold. Use the phrases from Exercise 1a.

Hi, Arline,

How are you? Everything's fine here at Los Alamos. You wouldn't believe some of the scientists I'm working with. There's Hans Vogel, who **is focusing on** particle theory. He has really **given everything of himself to** his research. He's probably one of the greatest scientists **in history**. There's also Bernheimer, **renowned for** his work in physics. He won the Nobel Prize for his contribution to nanotechnology. He's the world's greatest expert **in his area**. He is totally **focused on** his work, which is **the creation and production of** a new type of weapon. I've managed to speak to him **a few times**, and even though he's working in very tough conditions, he doesn't seem to feel the stress.

I've been able to **get motivated through** my contact with these people, and I really hope I can **do well in** my work here.

Love,

Richard

2 Ten words are missing. Add them to complete the conversations.

1. **A:** Didn't you just love that movie?
   B: As matter of fact, we thought it was a little boring.
2. **A:** Be honest, I don't like ballet much.
   B: Far as the skill is concerned I think it's wonderful, but I can't say I've seen much of it.
3. **A:** Isn't that CD wonderful?
   B: To tell you truth, I think it's a bit overrated.
4. **A:** That movie was kind long, wasn't it?
   B: Long? I fell asleep at least twice. It was endless!
5. **A:** Bye, Hiro! Anyway, Rosa, I was saying, that restaurant is fantastic.
   B: Mind, it's not exactly cheap.
6. **A:** So if you can get three tickets, that'd be great.
   B: Any rate, I'll get at least two, OK?
7. **A:** He wrote, directed, and starred in that play.
   B: Frankly, he more less did everything!
8. **A:** Sorry, Keith. I interrupted you.
   B: I was going to say was that I enjoyed the exhibition very much.

3 Circle the correct choices to complete the paragraph.

Most companies, on making a mistake, publicly deny it and privately say, "Oh, no! If only we _have/had/should have_ (1.) done this!" Venture capitalists, who help fund new businesses, spend half their lives wishing they _have poured/must have put/had poured_ (2.) money into one thing and not another. Not Bessemer Venture Partners. This company has an "anti-portfolio" website which lists the great opportunities they missed. The list contains some of the biggest names in business. _If only/Should/What if_ (3.) Bessemer had put money into an unknown company called Apple Computers? _Suppose/Supposed/Wishing_ (4.) they hadn't turned down eBay? At the time eBay sold stamps and comic books, and Bessemer didn't see the potential. If only they _must have been/had been/had be_ (5.) able to read the future! Bessemer also turned down Google before it was famous. So why does Bessemer admit these mistakes? According to the website, they _would rather/are rather/rather_ (6.) laugh at their errors than try to cover them up. It may also be a marketing ploy; new businesses _had rather/prefer/would rather_ (7.) go to a venture company that has a reputation for honesty and openness than one that doesn't. Our conclusion? It's _the right time/high time/the time_ (8.) other companies came out and admitted (or even laughed at) their own mistakes.

4 Put the letters in parentheses in the correct order to complete the paragraph.

Jackson Pollock's early paintings were _____ (1. fgitareivu), though never realistic. In the 1940s, his work became more _____ (2. asttacrb) and less _____ (3. tdaanilorit), until he reached his zenith in the drip paintings of the mid-1940s. These were truly _____ (4. vatan-rgdae), _____ (5. stgninnu) works, painted on a huge scale. Although critics called Pollock a barbarian because of his technique, and found the violence of both his life and work _____ (6. dibgsrniut), what is _____ (7. stgrniki) about Hans Namuth's documentary of him painting is that he seems completely _____ (8. tqnaiurl) as he dances around the canvas, dripping paint.

5 Cross out the ending that is NOT possible.

1. That type of art isn't _____.
   a. my kind of thing
   b. my cup of tea
   c. my liking

2. It became clear that the facts in the case were _____.
   a. indisputable
   b. without a doubt
   c. undeniable

3. Bearing in mind the circumstances, I _____.
   a. would consider to do that
   b. would agree to that
   c. suppose I might agree

4. That's what they say, but in my opinion, it's _____.
   a. questionable
   b. debatable
   c. unquestionably

5. People think he reached the North Pole, but it's not _____.
   a. 100% certain
   b. without a doubt
   c. clear-cut

6. Her paintings weren't universally popular, but the critic Herman Bowers was _____.
   a. a big favorite
   b. really into her work
   c. a big fan

7. Daniel is worried that I'm going to leave the company, but _____.
   a. there's no way I'd do that
   b. I wouldn't probably do that
   c. it's unlikely I'd be able to do that

8. Some people hated those art-house movies, but Mrs. Williams _____.
   a. really related to that type of thing
   b. had always admired them
   c. couldn't agree to them

UNIT 10
Expressing feelings

Vocabulary

Just a feeling . . .

1 Read what five people say about their feelings. Then write a sentence to summarize how each person is feeling. Use phrases from the box.

> down in the dumps   of two minds
> pleased with herself   wound up
> at her wits end

1. _____
_____
_____
_____

2. _____
_____
_____
_____
_____

3. _____
_____
_____
_____
_____

4. _____
_____
_____
_____
_____

5. _____
_____
_____
_____
_____

2 On a separate sheet of paper, write a response to each person in Exercise 1.

1 I'm not really enjoying my job right now, and I don't seem to have much time to go out either, so I don't feel like I'm really making the most of life. I often don't get home until 9:00 or so, and it's too late to cook, so I usually end up just eating cereal in front of the TV and then falling asleep. And then before I know it, it's time to go back to work again.

2 I can't understand why she hasn't called me yet. I mean, she said she would call as soon as she arrived, and it's been two days now. I can't help thinking that something must have happened. It's not like her to not even send a text message. I'm worried sick. I'm going to have to call the police.

3 It's a boy! We went to have the tests yesterday, and I'm so excited. I can't believe you can actually see the baby on the screen, with his little hands and feet and everything. I have a photo of him, and it is the most amazing feeling. I used to be afraid to be a mother, but I'm so proud of myself for making this decision. I can't believe how happy I am, and to think that in just a few months . . .

4 I can't believe it. It is so annoying. I have waited all this time to get an appointment with a specialist, months and months, and now they write a letter to say that that specialist can't treat me anyway, and I need to find someone else. I mean, why didn't they just say that before, six months ago?! We pay huge amounts of money to these doctors, and it makes me so angry when you can't even get a simple appointment.

5 I'm not really sure what I want to do. I could come just for the day, I suppose, but it's such a long trip that I don't know if it's worth it to drive all that way. On the other hand, it would be great to see you all again, and if I don't come now, I don't know when I'll have another chance. And it's been so long since we saw each other . . .

Grammar

3 Rewrite the sentences using the words in parentheses.

1. It wasn't really necessary for us to bring all this equipment. (need)

   _____

   _____

2. There is a good chance that they'll find out sooner or later. (bound)

   _____

   _____

3. I think it would be a good idea if we looked around the house first. (ought)

   _____

   _____

4. She will probably do well in the race. (likely)

   _____

   _____

5. I can't believe there is no easier way to do this. (must)

   _____

   _____

6. I've asked her a hundred times already, but she is refusing to change her position. (won't)

   _____

   _____

7. It's impossible for them to charge that much for a service. It's ridiculous. (can't)

   _____

   _____

8. It's likely that we'll bump into you at the party on Saturday. (might)

   _____

   _____

9. They ask you to take your shoes off before you go in. (supposed)

   _____

   _____

4 Circle the correct words to complete the sentences.

1. Tim's flight took over fifteen hours. He ____ be exhausted.

   a. is supposed to   **b.** is likely   **c.** must

2. If you don't speak Mandarin, you ____ accept the job.

   a. can't   **b.** are supposed   **c.** are bound

3. Nobody ____ to talk in the library.

   a. is bound   **b.** is supposed   **c.** can't

4. He's had the problem for weeks, but he ____ see a doctor.

   a. ought   **b.** won't   **c.** is likely

5. The housing office ____ to help you find somewhere to live.

   a. ought   **b.** can't   **c.** might

6. You didn't ____ to have it delivered. I could have picked it up myself.

   a. ought   **b.** might   **c.** need

Vocabulary

5 Complete the ad with words or phrases from the box.

tough times	work out	dwelling
challenges	outlook	optimistic
chances are	looking on the bright side	

Would you say that you tend to be more _____ (1.) or more pessimistic? When you go through _____ (2.), do you usually assume that things will _____ (3.) in the long run, or do you take a more negative view? If you think that you need a little help _____ (4.) and would like to work on thinking more positively, a new class at the Wellness Center might be just the thing for you.

   Our class will help you adjust your _____ (5.) on life, helping you to see the positives in situations, rather than the negatives. We will lead you through exercises designed to make you aware of your thought patterns. We will help you to look for solutions to problems instead of _____ (6.) on the negative aspects of a situation. _____ (7.), when you have completed our class, you will be much more likely to see your problems as _____ (8.) to be overcome, and you will have a healthier way of looking at your life.

Grammar

1 Rewrite each sentence using the word in parentheses.

1. It's impossible for it to have been Pete in that car. (can't)

   _____
   _____

2. There's no answer. Maybe they've gone to bed. (could)

   _____
   _____

3. You weren't looking where you were going. The car nearly killed you. (might)

   _____
   _____

4. I'm not sure that they're still in the city. I think they moved. (may)

   _____
   _____

5. I'm glad you came. It would have been impossible without you. (couldn't)

   _____
   _____

6. I can't find it anywhere, but I know it's here. (must)

   _____
   _____

7. Rick and June are undecided about whether to come to the wedding reception. (might)

   _____
   _____

8. Someone called and left a message. It's possible that it was Carmen. (may)

   _____
   _____

9. I can't believe you are serious. (must)

   _____
   _____

10. They're still not here. Maybe they got lost. (might)

    _____
    _____

Vocabulary

2 Put the letters in parentheses in the correct order to make adjectives to complete the sentences.

1. He was _____ about being asked to play in the band. (ldrihtel)

2. Her family are _____ about her name being published in the newspaper. (soruifu)

3. Emma was a little _____ by his directness. (kante bacak)

4. The people lining the streets were _____ when they caught sight of the celebrities. (citsceta)

5. Tiffany was absolutely _____ to him, and it hurt. (dirntfenief)

6. She's been so _____ since Patrick left her. (silermabe)

7. He was _____ in politics. (terenuetinsd)

8. Sid is _____ of heights. (frerietid)

9. When I found out how much money we'd made, I was absolutely _____. (blastabfredge)

10. When we heard the news we were _____. (scmurktudb)

11. Customers were _____ by the price increases. (tuadroge)

12. Sandy will be _____ to see you. (lehtdideg)

13. She was absolutely _____ that he had lied. (divil)

14. I'm _____ of spiders. (diterfipe)

15. She was really _____ about the way her father treated her. (spute)

Reading

3 Read the article on the next page. Check the feelings and emotions that are described.

____ anger   ____ boredom
____ ecstasy   ____ hurt
____ contentment   ____ frustration
____ fear   ____ jealousy
____ regret   ____ surprise

Revenge Can Be Bittersweet

(1) Lady Sarah Graham-Moon became a hero to jilted women everywhere when she became famous for gettting even with her unfaithful husband.

(2) According to Lady Sarah Graham-Moon, her second husband, Sir Peter Graham-Moon, had been unfaithful for years, but events came to a head in 1992, when he moved his girlfriend into the neighborhood in which they lived in Berkshire, in the south of England. Having been angry about his behavior for years, Graham-Moon planned her revenge carefully.

(3) For starters, she poured gallons of white paint on his BMW and cut the sleeves off 32 of his custom-made Savile Row suits, which cost approximately $1,600 each. She also cut up several of his pricey cashmere coats. She then deposited 60 bottles of rare wine from his extensive collection on the doorsteps of many of their neighbors.

(4) Lady Moon became an instant celebrity. She appeared on the Oprah Winfrey Show, wrote a column for a national British newspaper, wrote a book on getting even with unfaithful spouses, and started a club, called the Old Bags Club, to support women who had been abandoned by their husbands. Moon insists that the goal of the club is not to counsel revenge, though she believes that revenge, if not taken too far, can be therapeutic. The main goal of the club, she says is to help women regain their self-esteem and self-reliance. The women who dwell on the details of the unfaithfulness are the ones who need the most help,

she says. "They keep on hating the guy, and it does them more harm than him."

(5) Moon and her unfaithful husband got divorced, and she later found happiness living with David Denyer, a gamekeeper whom she met in the mid-1990s. Accustomed to aristocratic men like her ex-husband, Moon was pleasantly surprised by how straightforward, honest, and decent Denyer was. Though they had been raised in completely different circumstances, Moon and Denyer found that they were somehow very compatible. They lived together in her home and raised chickens and hunting dogs. Moon recalls that it was the first time that she had been truly happy.

(6) Unfortunately, Moon's happiness was not to last. In February 2006, Denyer died in a shooting incident. Though some experts thought it to be suicide, Moon strongly disagreed. "If David had wanted to kill himself, he would have done it properly," she was quoted as saying. She believes that he fell, causing his gun to go off accidently.

(7) Moon's one regret? Not marrying Denyer. He had asked her to, but she had said no, having already gone through two failed marriages. Though she is again on her own, Moon credits Denyer with restoring her self-confidence. She clearly misses him very much. Her eyes well slightly with tears as she discusses him but, like a true English aristocrat, she holds her emotions in check. "Death is all around us," she says. "It isn't very nice, but there's no use crying great crocodile tears."

4 Read the article again. Mark the statements true (*T*) or false (*F*).

_____ 1. Lady Sarah Moon felt happiness for the first time when she met her third husband, David.

_____ 2. Moon's second husband was unfaithful to her.

_____ 3. Moon destroyed her husband's expensive clothes.

_____ 4. She destroyed his expensive bottles of wine.

_____ 5. Moon and Denyer had similar childhoods.

_____ 6. Moon started a club to teach other women how to get revenge.

_____ 7. Moon disagrees with some experts on the cause of Denyer's death.

_____ 8. Moon has no regrets.

5 Would you have reacted similarly to Lady Sarah Moon if you had been in a similar situation? Explain your answer.

_____

_____

_____

_____

_____

_____

_____

_____

_____

_____

_____

_____

_____

_____

_____

_____

Reading

1a Read the excerpt from a short story. How would you describe Aaron's parenting style? _____

_____

Mine

Max parked his tricycle carefully on a small patch of shade alongside the spiked metal fence that surrounded the sprinkler area. The depressed rectangle of soft asphalt was the favored hangout of the pre-school set after the sprinklers had been shut off each day, and little ones were already screaming and scurrying about among the shrinking patches of wet ground under the glare of an intense sun. Behind Max, on a raised cement terrace, young men from the neighborhood played basketball and handball. To either side lay a stretch of benches where old people hunkered over grey checkerboard tables, and young children made the most out of the minimum of a playground. Max stepped back to survey his work. He measured the gap between wheel and curb with his eyes and admired the bright yellow and red Fisher-Price decals emblazoned on its fenders. Satisfied, his mind and eyes wandered through the park to the slides and swings beyond.

From a bench in the shade on the other side, Aaron gazed across at his son between paragraphs. He had been bringing Max to this park every Saturday afternoon for almost a year now, a ritual that they both enjoyed. A slight breeze quivered through the gray streaks in Aaron's black hair and rustled the glossy pages in his hands as he watched Max standing in the bright sunlight, mouthing quietly to himself and pointing contentedly toward the play area, a pint-sized tour guide to ghosts. Their eyes met and the corners of Max's mouth twisted into a grin. He did a steep bank to the left as he tip-toed full speed around the fence toward his father, landing smack between his knees, a hand setting on each. Aaron caressed the soft cinnamon blonde spikes on top of Max's head and returned to his reading.

"I'm thirsty," Max announced, squirmed quietly, stretching onto the tips of his toes.

"Thirsty?" Aaron repeated in lazy, mock surprise, biding for time that he might sit a bit longer enjoying the few shady breezes and the last few paragraphs on Congress's reaction to the president's new economic plan. Max fidgeted patiently.

It was between the last two paragraphs that Aaron happened to look up and see a chubby four-year old with Rita Hayworth sunglasses saddling up on the tricycle and taking off. Her dark face aglow, she banked steeply to the left as she careened full speed around the spiked metal fence. Entering the short ramp and steps down into the sprinkler area, she hit full throttle on the soft asphalt below. Sensing trouble, Aaron returned to his reading. Max turned and saw her doing figure eights behind the fence and he let out a shriek. "Mine!" his finger pointed at her in indignant accusation.

Aaron leaned forward and, observing the general scene in the sprinkler area, patted Max's tensed back. "It's okay, sweetheart. You're not riding it now. You can have it back when she's finished." He reassured himself as well with his caring voice and the calm reasoning of his own words.

"It's mine!" Max shrieked again, his foot stomping angrily on the final word, his finger pointing even more accusingly than before.

Aaron looked at his son's reddened face and once again at the girl. A woman he assumed to be her mother chatted nearby with a friend, sitting on the low gray cement wall that supported the spiked metal fence, their gold and magenta saris glistening in the bright sunlight. "Well why don't you go and ask her for it back?" Max stood silently for a moment between his father's knees, tensed, but deep in thought. "Go and tell her you want your tricycle back. Go ahead," Aaron's voice advised, soothing and gentle.

Max repeated again, "It's mine," his voice a softer whine, the anger on his face shifting to the confusion of the learner. He walked over to the entrance in the fence and hesitated a moment to look back at his father. He stepped inside and stopped at the bottom of the steps. In a tiny voice, full of apprehension, he mouthed the words. The girl continued blissfully on her spree.

b Answer the questions. Explain your answers.

1. How do you think Max feels when he is asking the girl for his bike?

2. How do you think Aaron feels about the way he handled the situation?

3. What would you have done if you were in Aaron's position?

4. How do you think the problem will be resolved?

Grammar

2 Add *would* or *wouldn't* to the sentences. Make any other necessary changes.

1. Aaron and Max come to the park every Saturday.
2. Sometimes Max ride his tricycle while Aaron read the paper.
3. Often young men play basketball nearby.
4. Aaron have gotten the tricycle back himself, but he wanted Max to learn how to resolve problems by himself.
5. You give me my tricycle, please?
6. The girl listen to Max.

3 Find the mistakes in the sentences and correct them.

1. He had always said that he will give me money.
2. The teacher wouldn't never smile at me.
3. Would you like follow me to my office?
4. The family moved to the countryside so that they would have had a better quality of life.
5. She warned us that the job would to be hard.
6. I'd have change jobs earlier if I had realize how easy it was.
7. No matter how hard they tried, the horse wouldn't to leave the stable.
8. Would you to turn the lights off when you've finished?

Reading and writing

4 Read about a childhood memory. Answer the questions on a separate sheet of paper.

1. What experience does she describe?
2. Has she always enjoyed exams?
3. Why was she good at exams when she was younger?
4. What was different about the exams she took when she was in college?

This is a test . . .

I think I might have been sort of a geek when I was very young, because I used to love taking tests, and not many people do that. But I think that's because I did a lot of acting, and so I used to study for tests in the same way that I learned my lines. So when it came to test time, I just wrote out the answers word for word. And that's why I found my ACTs pretty easy. It was only later in life, when I came to do things like university exams, where you have to apply theory, that I learned that you can't always get away with just learning things by memory. I remember that I got very stressed out for my college exams, and I certainly learned the lesson that starting review about three weeks before your exam is not a good idea. So, for me, childhood memories of tests were fun, and I always managed to do well, but later on in life it got a little bit more difficult.

5 Complete the expressions in **bold**. Then match them to the definitions.

____ 1. I think I might have been **sort of a** _____.

____ 2. I just wrote out the answers **word for** _____.

____ 3. It was only _____ **in life**, when I came to do things like . . .

____ 4. . . . that you **can't always** _____ **away with** . . .

____ 5. . . . just **learning things by** _____

____ 6. I got very _____ **out** for my college exams.

____ 7. I certainly _____ **the lesson** that . . .

a. write down every word exactly as you learned or read it
b. it is not sufficient
c. nervous and tense
d. someone who studies hard but doesn't fit in socially
e. learned from experience
f. studying and remembering just the hard facts
g. when I was older

UNIT 10
Review

1 Add one word to complete each sentence.

1. I'm ____ of minds as to whether or not to go to the concert.

2. He's been a little bit ____ in the dumps recently.

3. She was at her ____ end about failing the exam.

4. Try not to get so wound ____ about life. Take it easy.

5. I'm feeling pretty pleased ____ myself for passing my driving test.

6. Now all the tickets are sold out, so we're ____ kicking.

2 Circle the correct words to complete the sentences.

1. They're _____ call us while they're in town.
   - **a.** need to
   - **b.** bound to
   - **c.** might to

2. We _____ get home because the babysitter is waiting.
   - **a.** 're bound to
   - **b.** supposed to
   - **c.** ought to

3. It _____ an easy decision to make.
   - **a.** can't have been
   - **b.** couldn't to be
   - **c.** isn't bound to be

4. They _____ there earlier than we were expecting.
   - **a.** must have got
   - **b.** mightn't have
   - **c.** would got

5. She _____ us if we had to bring something.
   - **a.** is supposed tell
   - **b.** might tell
   - **c.** would have told

6. The house _____ need painting, because nobody has lived there for ages.
   - **a.** would have
   - **b.** can't have
   - **c.** is likely to

7. We _____ expected to do all the work by ourselves.
   - **a.** can't be
   - **b.** ought to
   - **c.** are likely to

8. We _____ reply to the invitation before July 31.
   - **a.** need
   - **b.** are supposed to
   - **c.** would have

9. I _____ bring the spare copies after all.
   - **a.** 'm likely
   - **b.** ought
   - **c.** didn't need to

3 One word in each sentence belongs in another sentence. Cross out those words and write them in the correct sentences.

1. He has a tendency to change on the negative.

2. I'm sure it will all work out well in the long bright.

3. Try looking on the people side.

4. Generally, I see problems as run.

5. There are various techniques you can use to dwell your thought patterns.

6. I tend to trust challenges.

4 Circle the correct choice.

1. We were *outraged/petrified/delighted* when she graduated from college with high grades. We had always hoped that she would do well.

2. He was *furious/ecstatic/delighted* when he realized his wallet had been stolen.

3. They were really *terrified/taken aback/ indifferent* when we told them the price. It was obviously a shock.

4. She was simply *thrilled/dumbstruck/ uninterested* when she received the flowers. You could tell by her huge smile.

5. I'm a little *delighted/flabbergasted/indifferent* toward classical music. It doesn't do anything for me.

6. Most days she felt *miserable/taken aback/ livid*, and longed to see her friends and family at home.

7. I told him all about what had been happening, but he was completely *outraged/uninterested/ ecstatic*. He just kept watching TV.

8. She was *terrified/livid/dumbstruck* that her parents would find out what she had been doing.

9. Katia was *livid/thrilled/ecstatic* when she saw the mess that the builders had left. She immediately called the company to complain.

5 Add *would* or *wouldn't* to the story where appropriate.

When I was younger, my parents were always busy. They had just started their own business, so they often had to go overseas and couldn't take care of my brother and me. When they went away on these trips, they send us to stay with my grandfather, a fruit farmer who lives in the foothills of the mountains. I was always happy when my mother told us we stay with Grandpa, since the time we spent at his house was always wonderful. The air there was fresh and clean, and the scenery was beautiful. There was no pollution. In the morning, I wake up and smell the grass and the flowers, and hear the birds singing their song. There was an orchard filled with fruit trees of many kinds, and we were always happy when our grandfather ask: "You like to help pick the fruit?" When the fruit was ripe, we could pick as much as we could eat. And when there was too much, we set up a fruit stand, and make good money selling the sweet fruit to passers-by.

My grandfather kept dogs and chickens, and took us for walks in the forest. Here he taught us the names of the plants, so that we know which were good to eat, which were useful for medicinal purposes, and which were toxic. He let us pick the plants until we could tell him what each one was. We learned so much when we were with him, more than we have learned by going to school. I have stayed there forever, if it were possible.

6 Write five sentences about the story, using *would* or *wouldn't*.

Ex: *When their parents went away, the boys' grandfather would take care of them.*

_____

_____

_____

_____

_____

English in Common 6
Extra Listening Audioscript

The Extra Listening Audio MP3 files and printable Activity Worksheets are provided in both the Student book *ActiveBook* disc and in the Teacher's Resource Book *ActiveTeach* disc. The link for each unit is found at the top of the Unit Wrap Up page. The audio files are also available at the end of the Audio Program CDs. The audioscripts are also available as printable files on *ActiveBook* or *ActiveTeach*.

UNIT 1

▶ 2.21

A: Good evening listeners. This is Mark Johnson, reporting from a base camp on the slopes of Mt. Everest, the world's tallest mountain at 8,850 meters, which is around 29,000 feet. There's no chairlift to the top, so if you want to reach the peak, both your body and your bank account had better be in very good shape! I've learned that a guided trek for four to seven people can cost up to 80,000 dollars per person! Why is it so expensive? Well, the price includes a lead guide at 25,000 dollars, 2 assistant guides at 10,000 dollars each, 3—4 cooks at 3,500 dollars each, a doctor at 4,000 dollars, high quality oxygen at 30,000 dollars, 150 yaks to transport equipment, and much more! Not to mention very pricey climbing permits and fees from the government of Nepal, and a garbage and human waste disposal fee of 4,000 dollars paid to the Sagarmatha National Park.

Today, I'm talking to a young mountaineer, Sunny Lee, a 30-year-old Korean-American climber. Sunny, I understand that this is the fifth of the fourteen tallest summits that you are attempting to climb. Why have you chosen Everest, and how have you raised the money to pay for the expedition?

B: Well, first, of course, I couldn't have gotten here without a lot of help. As you said, climbing is a very expensive sport. I'd like to thank my parents, my sponsors, and my many supporters. I've also been very lucky in raising funds—a TV production company is filming this climb, which covers most of the cost. Why am I here? Well, I've always wanted to climb Everest—like most people say, "Because it is there!"

A: What inspired you to take up this dangerous sport?

B: A Korean mountaineer, Oh Eun-Sun has been my inspiration—she's a fantastic climber, the number two woman in the world. I've learned a lot from her example.

A: Like what?

B: Well, mostly to be very careful. I never climb alone, for example—I don't want any accidents to happen. And I like to set attainable goals, so before starting, every detail of the climb is planned very carefully. My team knows where we'll be stopping each night, and what supplies we'll need. Base camps are set up in advance. Of course, Sherpa guides always climb alongside us.

A: What is your happiest climbing memory?

B: It's hard to say. There have been many wonderful times, but maybe the best was when I reached the top of the first mountain I climbed. It was Mt. Hallasan, in Korea. It's small compared to Everest, but I felt as if the world was at my feet.

A: What are your plans for the future? How long will you continue climbing?

B: I don't really know. I don't climb mountains to set records; I climb because I love the challenge. I'd like to keep climbing for a few more years, but I'd also like to spend more time with my family . . .

UNIT 2

A: So how was your trip around the world? You were gone for over three months.

B: Did you have a great time?

C: YES! I loved the sights, of course, but the best part was meeting people. We became couchsurfers and sometimes stayed in people's homes—free!

A: Couchsurfers? What's that? I've never heard of it before.

C: Well, the actual name of the organization is couchsurfers.org. It's a volunteer network of people who open their homes for a few nights to visitors. You may have a bedroom, or sleep on the couch in the living room. Your hosts set rules, like whether you can use their kitchen or washing machine. It's a fantastic way to make international friends.

D: It wasn't always as comfortable as staying in a hotel, but it was wonderful to see how people live. All of our hosts were glad to talk to us. Some also showed us around, and some included us in day-to-day chores like shopping and cooking.

C: And of course, they know great local restaurants and local sights that we would never find on our own.

B: You know, I just read a really interesting article in *Travel and Leisure* magazine about cultural mistakes that people make on their vacations.

C: I think we made a lot of them!

A: Like what?

C: Well, there was the time I used my left hand to eat couscous in Azerbaijan. Everyone looked at me so strangely. I didn't have a clue what I was doing wrong.

D: Yeah, later we found out why . . . our hostess whispered to us, "That's the bathroom hand."

A:/B: Uh oh!

C: I was so embarrassed.

D: Yeah, well what about that time in Japan when I put my arm around Noriko's shoulder? She gave me a very funny look. I learned not to do that again.

C: Yeah, but contrast that to our time in Brazil when I was introduced to Silvia's boyfriend. I was giving him my hand to shake, when he kissed me three times! That felt weird—but nice!

A: I guess you just have to observe what locals do. Different cultures have different comfort levels when it comes to personal space.

C: Yeah, and I also became aware of some unconscious habits Americans have.

A: Like what?

C: Like smiling at strangers! We think it's friendly, but French people think we're insincere.

D: But, you know, even within the same country, it's possible to offend people. Do you remember when we were in the Midwest, visiting our cousins?

A: What did you do wrong?

C: Well, Midwesterners usually say, "Hello" or "Good morning" when they pass someone on the street, even a stranger. New Yorkers are more apt to just walk on by without a greeting. We discovered that Midwesterners see that as being rude.

A: That's true! New Yorkers can be a little less than friendly!

D: Oh, I forgot, you're from the Midwest, too!

C: Well, the more we travel, the more we have to learn! We're already starting to plan our next trip . . .

UNIT 3

▶ 2.23

A: Good evening, everyone. I hope you're enjoying your time camping at our beautiful National Forest here in Minnesota. Our program tonight, around the campfire, will be story-telling. Now, how many of you have heard of Paul Bunyon?

Voices: I have.
No, who is he?
Was he a real person?

A: Was he a real person? Hmm. Well, most people say he was "larger than life." I guess you'll see if you agree after you hear a few of my stories. Here goes:

Well, Paul was born right around here. He was a VERY big baby—and he grew so fast that one week after he was born, he had to wear his father's clothes! By the time he was one, his mother sewed wagon wheels on his shirts for buttons, and boy did he have a big appetite. It is said that he ate 40 bowls of oatmeal every morning for breakfast! He got to be so tall and wide that he wasn't comfortable in a house, except maybe to sleep. It was natural that he became a lumberjack, with the great outdoors for his home.

Voices: I guess this is a "tall story."
Shhh. Let's listen!

A: In all our history, there has never been a lumberjack to equal Paul Bunyan! Why, he could cut down hundreds of trees single-handedly in just a few minutes by tying his huge ax to the end of a long rope and swinging it in circles. Now one year, here in the north, we had two winters! Yup, it snowed in winter and in summer, too. It was so cold that all the fish swam south. Milk turned to ice cream as it was being poured. And when people spoke at night, their words froze in mid-air! They had to wait until the next morning, when the sun came up, to hear the words as they defrosted!

B: Didn't Paul have a pet ox?

A: That's true. One day that winter, Paul was jogging through the snow to keep warm—by the way, that small lake over there is from one of his footprints—when he spotted a little ox almost hidden by the snow. The ox was blue with cold, and he stayed blue even when he warmed up. Paul named him Babe. Babe grew fast, and was soon huge and super strong.

Paul and Babe, his blue ox became quite a team—no work was too hard for them. Babe could haul the logs away as fast as Paul could cut them. Sometimes, though, it was difficult to get the tall logs out of the forest on twisty logging roads. So Paul tied the ends of the roads to Babe's horns, and Babe pulled those roads straight as an arrow . . .

UNIT 4

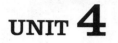 2.24

A: OK, folks, lunch is cleaned up. Chances are the kids won't get back from ice skating until around 4 o'clock. What should we do until then? Go for a walk? Read by the fire? Just sit and talk?

B: How about a game of Jeopardy? I've got the set right here.

C: Sounds like fun, Mike. Remind me of the rules.

B: Well, to start, I'll be the host and you three can be the contestants. Questions are worth between one hundred and 500 dollars, depending on difficulty. If you know the answer, push the buzzer. And remember, your answers have to be in question form. The categories in this round are children's books, inventions we use everyday, and the Olympics. Sally, will you keep score?

D: She'll probably cheat! We'd better watch her!

A: Oh shush! Stop teasing your sister, Bill! You know, I think you don't have a hope of winning with these categories unless she gives you extra points by mistake!

B: Are you guys ready? We'll start with children's books for one hundred dollars. This young woman fell through a rabbit hole and met a cat with a crazy smile.

D: Who is Alice in Wonderland?

B: Correct! Sally, give Bill one hundred dollars.

C: How did you get that question, Bill? You never read a book when we were little!

D: Did too!

C: You did not!

B: OK, children, it's time to grow up, or I'll send you to your rooms!

C:/D: We'll be good, promise!

B: Next, inventions for $300. This product was invented by Mary Anderson in 1903 to help streetcars operate safely in the rain.

A: What is a windshield wiper?

B: Correct, $300 for Lisa. Next question is Olympics for $400. By summer 2016, this city will have hosted the 31st Olympiad.

C: What is London?

B: Sorry. Wrong answer.

D: What is Rio?

B: Correct. $400 more for Bill. Looks like he's going to win. Next, inventions for $200. These little brown pieces of candy weren't invented until 1930. They revolutionized cookies in America.

A: What are chocolate chips?

B: Correct, Lisa. I was pretty sure you'd get that one, judging by the delicious smell wafting in here. Uh oh. Look at the time! We're going to have to finish up.

A: Sally, what's the score so far?

C: Bill is ahead by $200. You and I are tied. The next question may well be the decider.

B: Well, good luck everyone. And the last question is worth $500. This machine was patented in 1889 by Josephine Garis Cochran. A handle sprayed hot, soapy water into a tub. At first it was used only by some restaurants and hotels.

D: What is a dishwasher?

B: Correct! And the winner is Bill. Congratulations!

A: Good job, Bill!

C: You're smarter than I thought, kid brother! Well done!

A: OK! Who'd like some coffee and chocolate chip cookies?

All: Me, I would! Me, too . . .

UNIT 5

▶ 2.25

A: Good morning, listeners. Steve Ross here on *Talking Business*, Radio WAMB. Today, my guest, entrepreneur Ellen Simpson, and I are going to discuss business reactions to the uncertain economic times we're living in these days. Ellen, how are most large corporations dealing with smaller profits, or the fear that banks may fail?

B: Unfortunately, Steve, a lot of them have stopped hiring new workers, so those that remain have to work harder. At the same time, there's less opportunity for promotion and higher salaries for the employees that they already have. This leads to more stress for these workers and less job satisfaction. And if people are afraid of losing their jobs, they begin to spend less on nonessential purchases. So profits go down even more. It's a vicious cycle. And many of our big corporate leaders and CEOs have expressed their concern about the need for more cooperation and responsibility among elected officials. They want the USA to be on a firm fiscal footing. That's important for business growth and investment.

A: What about fringe benefits that workers have become accustomed to? A lot of my friends, especially younger women with children, say that the gains made by their mothers—like flexible working hours and money for childcare or professional development—are disappearing. Is that true?

B: Broadly speaking, it is true. A lot of businesses are looking to save money by cutting benefits. Pensions especially, are being attacked as too expensive to sustain.

A: Do you think this is a long-term trend?

B: Yes, I do. There are some companies, of course, that remain committed to sharing their success with employees through the extras we used to take for granted, like health care, 401K retirement plans, and tuition reimbursement, but the packages are less generous than they used to be. If only more business leaders would realize that benefits are correlated to job satisfaction. . . .

A: And job satisfaction to productivity! I really believe in tuition reimbursement for young workers. It's a strong incentive for continuing to learn new skills.

B: I agree!

A: So, what do you predict for the future, Ellen? Is this just a small dip in our economic fortunes, or is the world headed into another bad recession?

B: If I had a crystal ball, Steve, I might be able to answer that question! I do think we're headed in the wrong direction, though. In hindsight, if we had spent more money on creating jobs two years ago, we might not be in this mess now.

A: Thank you Ellen. Listeners, let's hear from you now. Have any of you . . .

UNIT 6

▶ 2.26

A: Hi Kate. Wake up! The library's closing. Time to go home.

B: Huh? Oh, hi, Dan. Sorry! I wasn't sleeping. Just deep in thought. I'm trying to figure out a subject to research for my sociology paper.

A: What's the topic?

B: We have to write about an inspirational or charismatic leader, maybe someone who led his country in wartime, or through a difficult economic period.

A: That shouldn't be difficult. Just Google "world leader" . . .

B: Don't be silly! Anyway, I did that and thousands of pages came up! I want to research someone who doesn't waver in the face of problems, who is tireless in fighting for what he or she believes in, and who is also approachable.

A: In other words, a pretty unusual person. Like Mahatma Gandhi?

B: Uh-huh. But too many people have already chosen him. I want to be different.

A: Probably a good idea—you don't want your professor to compare your research with others.

B: Also, whoever I choose has to be incorruptible as well—so many political leaders look good until you dig deep, and find that, in spite of what they say, they are secretly indebted to lobbyists or special interest groups.

A: You're right. Look at the recent scandals in the UK, for example. Didn't a politician get implicated in a media ethics scandal?

B: In any case, the topic is just too big. I don't know where to start.

A: How long does the paper have to be?

B: My professor said to make it as long as necessary to do justice to the topic! However, I'd like to keep it under twenty pages—about 5,000 words.

A: Well, start by making a list of possible subjects, or time periods. Do you want someone who is still living, or someone who died in the last century? Or a much older historical figure?

B: Mmm. Someone from long ago would be easier to research than a current leader. Maybe someone like Elizabeth the First of England. She always put her country first. I'm not sure how approachable she was, though.

A: Well, she certainly knew how to make tough decisions. Didn't she have her cousin, Mary Queen of Scots beheaded?

B: Yeah, remember that scene in the movie? I couldn't watch the execution. What a horrible decision to have to make!

A: Yeah, but it was to save her throne! Well, whoever you choose, try to find just one or two events that show how he or she acted when under stress and analyze those.

B: Good advice. I'll get started first thing tomorrow morning. Now, how about getting something to eat?

UNIT 7

▶ 2.27

A: Good morning, everyone. Welcome to the West coast job fair for applicants who are interested in working on "The Ice"—that is in Antarctica—at one of our permanent stations, in a field camp, or on a research ship. As you probably already know, conditions there are challenging. You'll be on duty six or even seven days a week working in unpredictable weather, with average temperatures around zero degrees Celsius, or 32 degrees Fahrenheit, even in the summer. Any questions so far? No?

OK. As our recruitment materials make clear, most of our scientists are military, or university professors on research grants. Civilians, like you here today, are mainly hired for support services. I want to stress that everyone on the team is important! Without people who can cook, clean, and fix broken machinery and computers, our astrophysicists and astronomers could not succeed in their important work. I see a hand up in the back. What's your question, sir?

B: Actually, I'm here with my daughter, as a concerned Dad. I'd like to know why you, a young woman, went to Antarctica? Weren't you very lonely?

A: Good question! I went mostly for personal adventure! But I was pleasantly surprised to learn that nearly half of the staff at McMurdo station, where I was based, are female, including our base commander, and some of the leaders of scientific teams. Your daughter will be fine.

B: Thank you!

A: Yes? The woman in front . . .

C: What do the staff do during the dark months?

A: I myself overwintered there for six months last year, so I can fill you in on what the "Big Dark" was like. Of course, we continued focusing on research projects, but it was quieter, with only about 50 people instead of around 200. There was more time for reading, relaxation—we have a library and three TV channels—and exercise. I remember my first time skiing over miles of completely clean snow that sparkled like diamonds in the moonlight. Next question . . . Yes? The gentleman in the third row?

D: I have two questions. First, what happens if you get sick?

A: Well sickness, of course, can be a problem. We do have a physician who remains with us during the winter and stays in contact with other doctors through the internet for advice. And we stock an excellent pharmacy for routine illnesses. It's almost impossible to get supplies dropped in, although in 1999, the station's overwintering doctor, Jerri Nielsen, discovered that she had breast cancer. There was a daring July drop of chemotherapy supplies for her.

D: And food? What do you eat when you can't bring in fresh supplies?

A: The station has a small greenhouse. We grow a variety of vegetables and herbs, hydroponically, without soil, using only water and nutrients. Most fruits have to come frozen or in cans, of course. Some of you here might be assigned as gardeners! Any more questions? No? Then let me conclude by saying . . .

UNIT 8

▶ 2.28

A: Good afternoon, listeners. I'm Alison Berlin, and this is *Issues in the News*. Today my two guests are on opposing sides of proposals to allow deep-sea drilling off the northern coast of Alaska. Stuart Ross, your firm represents some of the big oil companies that are pushing for Increased exploitation of Alaskan oil. Is that environmentally safe?

B: Yes, indeed, Alison. In the last few years, we've developed several innovative technologies that will allow us to drill with much less damage to the ocean.

A: For example?

B: Well, one is called "through-tube" drilling. A new well is drilled through the production tubing of an older well. Not needing to redrill, or pull out the old tubes, can potentially save about one million dollars in labor costs. Let me stress that the benefits of achieving energy independence through increased production of domestic oil are worth the risks.

A: Brian Adams, what do you think?

C: Alison, the fact of the matter is that the environment can't tolerate deep sea drilling. Let's remember that the BP blowout in the Gulf of Mexico took five months to get under control. One hundred seventy million gallons of crude oil poured into the gulf, and it will take years to clean up the mess. The shrimp industry was almost destroyed, not to mention the thousands of birds and fish that died. And we still don't know what the long-term effects on the environment will be.

A: Are you saying that it's irresponsible to drill in the Beaufort Sea, off the North Slope of Alaska?

C: Yes, I am. We're just not technologically ready to risk Arctic waters and the pristine ecosystem that exists there. The oil companies have admitted that they don't know how to cope with leaks that occur miles under the ocean floor. We're talking about a location that's blocked in by ice for eight months of the year, and one thousand miles away from Coast Guard help.

A: Stuart Ross, would you like to comment on these points?

B: Yes, thank you. I understand the issues that my fellow guest has brought up. The fact remains, however, that our country and the world are dependent on oil today and will remain so for the foreseeable future. We need additional sources of energy! And, of course, development of new oilfields means more jobs and tax revenue, both of which we sorely need.

A: Can you expand on that?

B: Studies have shown that allowing drilling in Alaska could generate 1.4 million new jobs by 2030, along with 800 billion dollars in additional revenue for the government. By the way, our own domestic consumption will probably remain about the same in the next 20 years, so we'll see a big drop in the amount of oil we need to import.

C: I'd much rather we spent our time and money on developing alternative, clean energy sources, like wind and solar power! Those could create jobs as well!

A: I'm afraid that time is up. Thank you gentlemen for your insightful analysis of a controversial issue.

B: Thank you.

C: Thank you.

UNIT 9

▶ 2.29

A: Good afternoon. Today's art history lecture will focus on a controversial topic, "Graffiti Art." I am aware that many people, and most police and public officials, consider graffiti to be a form of vandalism, a crime that should be punished. Frankly, if someone's name in black spray paint appeared on my freshly painted garage door, I would probably agree and be very annoyed. However, as an art historian, I have a broader view of the subject. I think that it's time for us to start appreciating that art is found all around us, and not only in museums.

Graffiti is not, in fact, new. It has existed for at least 2,500 years, with examples commonly found on ancient Egyptian temples and on the walls of buildings in Pompeii and Rome, including Latin curses and political slogans. At any rate, modern graffiti art began in the United States in the late 1960's, with the invention of permanent markers and spray paint. Some people believe that it started as a way to express political and social anger, a part of hip-hop culture, and is closely related to rap music.

Although it may have started as a form of rebellion, graffiti has crossed over into the mainstream art world. Exclusive galleries in Europe have shown works on canvas by graffiti artists. Artists you may have heard of include Keith Haring, whose designs on t-shirts and bags had first been seen spray-painted on city walls, and the French crew 123Klan, a group of artists that has produced logos, illustrations, and designs for Nike, Coca Cola, and Sony among other corporations. I think you'll agree that that is definitely mainstream!

I see that some of you are shaking your heads. Let me backtrack for a minute. Not all graffiti is art, of course. In the early days, teens simply sprayed their initials and part of their street address, all over subway cars, kind of a competition to say "I was here; notice me." We call this "tagging." At first the tags were monochromatic, in only one color. Later they became more elaborate and creative. But was this art? I would say, "Not yet."

In my opinion, graffiti became art when it became less spontaneous. Today's artists often start out with a sketch, decide on colors, and plot out the size of their design. They want to communicate feelings and ideas to as many viewers as possible, and so choose a public location, like the side of a building or highway wall. Of course, when a graffiti artist paints without permission, his or her work can be legally removed, sometimes by the next day. Still, just because the work is not hanging on a museum wall, doesn't mean it is not art.

To sum up, all new forms of art shock! Think of how your grandparents reacted to Picasso's cubist portraits. Or how their grandparents felt when looking at an impressionist landscape by Monet. That's how New Yorkers must have felt when they stepped inside of rainbow-colored subway cars back in the 1970s—I wish I had been there.

UNIT **10**

▶ 2.30

A: Hi, I'm Carol, a roving reporter for our local newspaper, *The Sun*. My topic for today is "Happiness." Would you be willing to share your thoughts and a memory or two with me?

B: Sure. I'd be happy to.

A: I've heard that one before!

B: Sorry. Well, I think happiness is determined by your outlook on life.

A: How so?

B: Well, I tend to look on the bright side of things. For example, I don't particularly like my long commute to work, and I wish I had a higher salary, but I'm really happy to have a job! It took me a year to find one in my field after I graduated from college.

A: Were you miserable while you were job hunting?

B: Not really. I'm pretty much an optimist. I was sure that I'd find something sooner or later, and I did. Luckily, I was able to live at home with my folks while I job-hunted. And I'll be even happier when I've saved enough money to move out!

A: What is your earliest happy memory?

B: Uh, I guess I was around four years old. We always went to my grandparents' house on a lake for a week or two in the summer. My father was trying to teach me to swim, in very shallow water, but I was terrified of getting my face wet.

A: Mmm, I can relate to that. I'm still not a good swimmer.

B: You should take lessons! Anyway, my father was at his wits end, trying to make me relax. Then he saw a school of small golden fish swimming by, and pointed them out to me. I wanted to see them more clearly, took a breath, and put my face in the water. I can still remember how pleased I was with myself when I realized I could do something that had frightened me. It was a good life lesson.

A: And another memory, as you got older?

B: Mmm. I have to think. . . . Oh, OK. Of course! It was in college. Looking back, it's hard to believe that I had the nerve to try out for the basketball team. As you can see, I'm only 5'9" — not nearly as tall as most of the players. But I loved the game. Luckily, not too many people wanted to play that year.

A: And?

B: Well, the coach was impressed with my shooting ability. Actually, he was flabbergasted that I could make a basket from halfway across the court. It was the happiest day of my life when he put me on the team.

A: Did you play a lot?

B: Actually, no . . . I sat on the bench most of the time. But I learned a lot from him about coaching, and now I volunteer at a local school with special-needs kids. I have a great time with them.

A: It sounds like you're a really positive person. Thanks for letting me interview you.

B: You're welcome. Um . . .

A: Yes?

B: It would make me very happy if you'd have a cup of coffee with me.